THE STORY OF TY COBB:
Baseball's Greatest Player

Gene Schoor
with
Henry Gilford

Illustrated with
photographs

AN ARCHWAY PAPERBACK
POCKET BOOKS • NEW YORK

THE STORY OF TY COBB

Julian Messner edition published 1952

Archway Paperback edition published November, 1967
4th printing .... October, 1973

L

Published by
POCKET BOOKS, a division of Simon & Schuster, Inc.,
630 Fifth Avenue, New York, N.Y.

Archway Paperback editions are distributed in the U.S.
by Simon & Schuster, Inc., 630 Fifth Avenue, New
York, N.Y. 10020, and in Canada by Simon & Schuster
of Canada, Ltd., Richmond Hill, Ontario, Canada.

Printed in the U.S.A.

FIRST LICK IN THE MAJORS!

Ty tapped the plate with his bat, looked out to the mound and swung menacingly at the pitcher.

Chesbro looked back at second, where Lindsay stood waiting to be moved on. The pitcher toed the rubber and sent a fast one across the plate. Ty swung and missed.

"Strike one!"

Chesbro glanced back to second, fired again to the plate. Cobb watched it go by.

"Strike two!" bawled the umpire.

Chesbro didn't bother looking back to second. He wound up, snapped the ball in and the young Georgian met it—hard. The pellet shot on a line past the center fielder, and Tyrus Raymond Cobb raced to first, turned and sped toward second, slid into the dust and made it. Lindsay had scored, Ty Cobb had made his first hit in the major leagues—his first double—and had batted in his first run. It was a suitable debut for the Georgia Peach.

THE STORY OF TY COBB:
Baseball's Greatest Player
was originally published
by Julian Messner.

Critics' Corner:

"Schoor surely has the knack of re-creating the incidents in the life of his famous subject with all the freshness and vividness, as though he had just observed them. Excellent reading."   —*Library Journal*

"This is an excellent biography of a great American sportsman, and a history of baseball from the early years of the century to today."   —*Saturday Review*

"An interesting, informative, and inspirational story about one of baseball's greatest players. . . . This book should be a welcome addition to any sports library."
—*Catholic Schools Journal*

Other Recommendations: A.L.A. Booklist; A.L.A. Basic Book Collection for Elementary Grades; Bro-Dart Foundation, Elementary School Library Collection; H. W. Wilson Standard Catalog for High School Libraries.

About the Author:

GENE SCHOOR was born in Passaic, New Jersey, and graduated from high school a four-letter man in football, baseball, basketball, and boxing. He won fifty-two out of fifty-five boxing bouts during his collegiate career at the University of Miami. After graduation, he was boxing coach at the University of Minnesota and then came to New York City, where he taught boxing and health education at CCNY and NYU. He has done newspaper and radio work; has produced sport shows with such famous people as Joe DiMaggio, Jack Dempsey, Phil Rizzuto; and has written many biographies of sports personalities.

PUBLISHER'S NOTE: Ty Cobb was born on December 18, 1886 and died on July 17, 1961.

TO FRAN

Who loves the game
and can keep score, too

ACKNOWLEDGMENT

Many thanks to Furman Bishler, Sports Editor of the Atlanta Constitution, for research on the early life of Ty Cobb; to Sandy Palmer, Miami Beach; Max Kantor; Fran Schoor; Virginia Lee Rose, for editorial assistance.

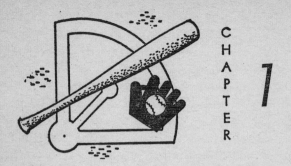

BIG, redheaded John Yarborough sat on the bench, watching his Royston Rompers take the field. He watched serious-faced Stewart Brown wind up in the pitcher's box, taking his warm-up tosses to the plate. He looked at sturdy Bob Mc-Crary, hunched behind home, peg the ball easily across the diamond to second base. It was a good nine he had put out on the grass, a hustling, fighting, spirited, winning nine, as good a ball club as a small town like Royston could boast. Brother John—that was what everyone in the town called him—was well satisfied with his congregation of teen-age ball players and had every reason to be. Not only did he have a winning team, he also had a good Sunday-school attendance.

Brother John was a ballplayer—and a good one at that—long before he had become a minister. He had been a first-rate man with the mask for Richmond Academy and a terror with the bat. He was a good minister—there was no doubt of that.

1

And he remained a minister despite all the offers to lure him into the national pastime of swatting a small ball over the fences. But Brother John knew his baseball, too. He knew what made a player tick. He also—and this proved most important to the history of the game—knew a ballplayer when he saw him.

He watched Stewart Brown throwing them into the plate, and Bob McCrary tossing the ball down to second, but his eyes were glued on the twelve-year-old boy pawing the dirt in the shortfield.

The boy caught the brother's eye. The brother smiled but not the boy. He wasn't a smiling youngster, not with the game in the fifth inning and the Royston Rompers behind in a five-three ball game.

He was the youngest teen-ager on the team. He was three or four inches shorter than anyone else on the club and twenty pounds lighter. By everything that could be measured in numbers, the shortstop of the Royston Rompers should have been somewhere in the stands watching the ball game. But there are things that aren't measured by numbers and it was in these things that the twelve-year-old infielder was on the top rung of the ladder, all by himself.

Brother Yarborough looked at the boy shouting at his pitcher.

"All right there, Stew! Just toss them in! They're blind as bats in your father's barn! Put it in there, Stew! They can't see 'em! Left their glasses home!"

He was a cocky kid, sure of himself, sharp tongued, belligerent, unafraid, aggressive.

2

Just a fight waiting for someplace to happen, thought John Yarborough.

Stewart Brown took his windup and threw one into the plate.

"Ball one!" called the umpire standing behind the pitcher.

"Wow!" protested the shortstop, throwing his glove into the air. "Let 'em hit it, Stew! Let 'em hit it. Ball!" he bellowed. "The guy can't see!"

He had walked right up to the umpire—to make sure he heard everything—and the umpire looked down belligerently from his six-foot height at the snorting youngster.

"Want my job?" he asked the boy.

The boy's eyes burned with antagonism.

"Call 'em right!" he shouted and went back to his position.

Brother Yarborough just watched, controlling his grin. The kid played the game as if he were in the big leagues.

Stewart Brown took his windup.

"Let 'em hit it!" yelled the kid in the shortfield, and the batter did!

It wasn't a hard-hit ball but it was well enough hit to fall where the second baseman couldn't catch up with it and the right fielder couldn't quite reach it. Now there was a man on first and the boy in the shortfield was tearing up the ground with his spikes.

"Come on, Stew! Come on, boy!"

Stewart Brown took his windup, threw the ball fast into the plate.

Again the click of the bat meeting the ball and the ball skipping like a bullet through the mound, and the runner from first racing for second.

But this time there was someone to meet the ball. Moving with the crack of the bat, far to his left, was the kid shortstop. A scoop out of the dirt, a tag on the runner coming down and a quick toss to first—and there were two out.

The young shortstop started to move back to his fielding position.

"That was my ball," said the second baseman of the Royston Rompers.

"Two out, aren't there?" answered the kid fielder.

"But that was my ball!" insisted the second baseman.

"Then you should have got it!" snapped the cocky shortstop, and that was the end of the argument.

Brother John, sitting on the bench, stroked his chin thoughtfully, thinking how best to cope with this young wildcat, and how best to smooth down the irritation of his second baseman. This wasn't the first time and it wouldn't be the last time that the boy would have to be reminded of the area he was supposed to cover.

"What position are you playing?" he asked the twelve-year-old, when the Rompers came into the bench for their licks.

"Shortstop," said the youngster.

"Looks like you played second this inning," said Brother John.

The youngster turned on him sharply, his chin jutting, his face bristling.

"I got two out, didn't I?"

"And in the last inning," said Brother Yarborough, quietly, "you almost knocked our third baseman out of the game, cutting in front of him like he wasn't there at all."

"He wasn't!" snapped the shortstop.

"Look," said the big brother, patiently. "There are nine men on a ball team. Nine." He held up the fingers to show nine on his hands. "You're only one of them. You play your field. Let the others play theirs."

The youngster didn't answer. He couldn't. The tears filled his eyes and ran down his cheeks.

But they weren't tears of contrition. There was no sorrow in the young boy. He wasn't asking for any forgiveness. He wasn't saying, "I won't do it again, Brother John."

And Brother John knew it.

These were tears of anger, of bitterness—almost hate. The boy with the tears in his eyes was no lamentable figure but a youngster far older than his twelve years, and capable of a physical outburst which would put to flight boys much older than he. There was wrath and fury in the boy's tears and Brother Yarborough knew only one way to meet it.

"Let's see what you can do with your bat," he said and turned away.

There was no sense in pursuing the argument. The boy would continue to play ball in the same way. But the anger—the antagonism—had to be turned into some more profitable direction. The most profitable direction at that particular moment was against the team beating Royston five-three.

He was no bigger at the plate than he was in the field but his opponents had learned to respect him.

The first pitch was wide. The second pitch cut the plate and the shortstop swung at it and missed.

"Strike!" called the umpire.

The young shortstop took the call as a personal insult.

"I missed it!" he yelled at the umpire.

"By a mile," said the catcher behind the plate.

The kid infielder glared at him.

"Watch this!" he roared.

The ball was high and inside but the youngster was mad enough to climb a ladder to hit at that ball and he met it with all the power in his small body.

Off he went—not as fast but almost as fast as the flight of the baseball—around first and straight for second. The right fielder had come in fast, taken the ball on a short hop, whipped it into second and the second baseman had the pellet, waiting for the oncoming Romper. But he never got him.

In a cloud of dust and hooking a corner of the bag, the kid shortstop tore under the second baseman's reaching glove.

"Safe!" called the umpire.

The youngest of the Rompers got onto his feet, dusted down his uniform.

"You betcha!" he said.

He didn't grin at the dumbfounded second baseman. He sneered at him and he was satisfied.

The Royston Rompers from Georgia went on to win that game nine to six, but the game itself was not the most important win of the season. That is, it was not the most important win to anybody except to the kid shortstop. To the youngster who played the game as if his very blood depended on it, every game was the most important game. He would as soon lose an arm as lose a game. Nothing in the world was more important than coming home the winner. And nothing in the world was more important than baseball.

It wasn't that way in the beginning. There had been other ideas, other ambitions. At one time he had wanted to become a doctor. He had dreamed of becoming a great surgeon. But that was before he had tasted the fight and the fury of the diamond. That was before he had put on a glove and swarmed all over the infield. That was before he had picked up a bat and laced out a two-bagger over the fingers of the reaching third baseman's mitt. That was before he had cut around the bags, stretching a single into a double, a double into a triple. That was before he had stolen home under the pitcher's nose.

Then it became baseball, baseball and nothing but baseball, morning, noon and night.

"You'd rather play ball than eat," said the admiring Brother John.

"Yes, sir."

7

"You're a mighty good ballplayer," admitted the smiling, still pensive Brother Yarborough.

"I know," said the youngster, without breaking stride.

And he was all that. He was that at twelve and he was that for many years—a great player, perhaps the greatest player that was ever listed on a ball club's roster, Number One in the Baseball Hall of Fame in Cooperstown, New York.

The name of that youngster who played for Brother John Yarborough's Royston Rompers when he was no older than twelve was Tyrus Raymond Cobb. He was called Ty Cobb—the Georgia Peach, Ty Cobb.

STEWART BROWN was pitching them in and Ty
Cobb was batting them out. Right from the very
beginning, the young Georgia Peach knew that the
game of baseball was both a science and an art.
Like a scientist, he studied every part of the game,
every phase of it, every movement. There was
nothing about hitting, fielding, running that didn't
claim his most earnest study and attention. Even
the shape of the ball was important—and hour after hour he carved away making baseball bats at
Joe Cunningham's father's furniture shop.

But knowing the fine points of the game wasn't
enough. Theory without practice is no more profitable than practice without theory, and the young
Cobb knew that, too. If it wasn't Stewart Brown
pitching them in to him, it was someone else of
the Royston Rompers on the pitching mound. If
he wasn't hitting, he was out in the infield playing
them off the grass, or in the outfield shagging
flies. His mother never had to ask him where he

had gotten the dirt all over his face, or where he had gotten the fresh rip in his pants. She knew he had been out there in the field somewhere, had fashioned himself a sliding pit and had been practicing for hours on end, perfecting some new kind of slide into first or second or third or home.

Tyrus Raymond Cobb loved the game so much that it was difficult for him to understand how a fine pitcher like Stewart Brown was going to give it up, just to go on to some college.

"You could get a job with Atlanta easy," he said, watching young Stewart Brown wind up.

The ball should have hooked inside but Tyrus stepped in and cuffed it out into short center before the curve broke.

The center fielder broke for the ball but not fast enough.

"Wake up there, Johnny!" called Cobb. "You'll never get 'em if you wait till they're up in the air!"

The fielder retrieved the ball, tossed it back to Brown and Brown walked the ball back to Bob McCrary.

"No more today," he said.

"Tomorrow?" asked Cobb, eagerly.

Brown smiled.

"I'm afraid not."

He put his arm around Cobb. Tyrus was a big fellow now. He was seventeen and getting out of high school.

"You used to want to be a doctor yourself," said Stew Brown.

10

Cobb shook off the hand on his shoulder. He scowled.

"You go ahead and become an old sawbones," he snapped. "I'll be up there playing ball for Atlanta."

He looked at the serious-faced Brown sharply, as if going to medical school was perpetrating some kind of treason. Giving up a career in baseball was tantamount to treason, the way Tyrus saw things. It was the one thing he could never forgive in Big John Yarborough. How could a man cast away the glory of the diamond for anything resembling medicine or the ministry? He couldn't understand it. He didn't even try. It was baseball and nothing but baseball for Tyrus Raymond Cobb of Royston, Georgia.

But that wasn't the way they saw it at home, neither his father nor his mother nor—though he never asked them—his brother Paul and sister Florence. The baseball fervor which burned deeply into the core of the young Georgia Peach burned there alone, when he was at home with his family. And it burned there despite the cold water the rest of the Cobb family tried to pour on it.

Herschel Cobb, sire of the Cobb household, was of tough, stern stock. Originally he had come to Georgia out of the western stretch of North Carolina. His ancestors had come from England, like so many of the people from Georgia, crossing the wild Atlantic in wind-driven boats to cut their way through the wilderness of the New World. Freedom was the cry of the people, and there was no hardship too great, no obstacle so overbearing, that they were not prepared to meet and conquer it for the sake of personal, political and religious liberty.

Herschel Cobb was several generations removed from those first men who hewed the wood out of the forests for their homes and drew the first clean waters out of the earth, but much of the spirit and the will of his forebearers remained with him.

He married Amanda Chitwood who, as stories have it, was part Indian, and settled long enough in Narrows, Georgia, to await the arrival of his first son. Narrows was—and still is—one of those tiny rural communities which dot the American landscape, a general store with a hole of a window for the United States mails, and a scattering of farmhouses. Nothing more. Nobody except the few inhabitants of the place on the edge of Banks County and just a jump from the Carolina borders would have heard of it. And it might just as easily have passed away without notice, except for one event, the birth of a child to Herschel and Amanda Cobb, on December 18, 1886. They named the child Tyrus Raymond Cobb, and in the history of baseball, with the possible exception of Cooperstown, New York, there is no more important location in the United States.

But the Cobb family did not stay very long in this illustrious hamlet. They picked up and moved on to Carnesville, the county seat of the neighboring county of Franklin. Here again their stay was short, and the restless Herschel had them on the move again in short order, this time to Royston, ten miles away. Here the elder Cobb finally settled— and it was from Royston that Herschel Cobb contributed his good share to the development of Georgia.

For a while the head of the Cobb family served his district as the elected representative in the Georgia Senate, and he served well, bringing credit not only to Royston and its surrounding area but to the state as well. Herschel Cobb introduced legislation to set up a system of country schools throughout the state of Georgia. Like his pioneering ancestors he put his whole heart and soul into the project which would benefit all the people, all his neighbors, all his fellow citizens. He gave up the promising career which politics held for him and plunged into the fight to carry out successfully the huge state-wide school project.

"I believe, and I believe nothing more earnestly," he said, "that education is the cornerstone on which we build our democracy."

When the bill was passed, he eagerly accepted the job of superintending the establishment and development of schools in Hart County, and as superintendent he was an example of tireless purpose and activity.

"Fessor," they called Herschel Cobb. All men who had important educational jobs in Georgia were called "fessor" and Herschel never objected to the shortening of the word "professor," nor did he ever disown the title. He enjoyed it.

"Nothing in the world is more important than

a good education," he announced to his son Tyrus and Tyrus, whose fervor, single-mindedness, earnestness and eagerness went in another direction, knew that the main obstacle to his career in baseball was his equally stubborn, equally determined father.

"Why don't you go and see the Judge," said Herschel.

The son looked at the father. They had had another of a long series of verbal collisions.

"You are going to go to college!" the older Cobb had insisted. "You're going to go into a profession."

"But, sir!" the younger Cobb had argued. "Baseball *is* a profession. A good profession!"

"For hoodlums and gamblers and drunks!" the fessor had countered, and not without a knowledge of the game as it was played at the very beginning of the 1900's.

Tyrus bit his lip. He had had the answer for that, too. He had reeled off a list of impeccable names, men like Christy Mathewson, men who were a credit to any sport, any field of life endeavor they might have chosen. It had done no good. The elder Cobb was fixed in his ideas and fixed in his purpose. He was a wall, a stone wall, and there was no denting it.

"Go see the Judge!"

That was the way every argument ended. The judge was a good friend of Herschel Cobb's.

"Go see the Judge!"

He had seen the judge more times than he cared to remember. The story was always the same.

14

"Law is a beautiful profession, a brilliant profession. It needs young blood like yours, Tyrus. You'll make good, I know."

The judge took out all his lawbooks, read passage after passage to the fretting young man.

"But I want to be a ballplayer, sir! Nothing else. Can't you understand, sir? Can't you make father understand? I want to play ball, sir!"

"You'd make a mighty fine lawyer, Tyrus. A good judge, too, I'm thinking."

It was always the same. They were bouncing him from one dead end to another—and if his father wouldn't give way an inch in his determination to keep the young Tyrus out of baseball, the judge certainly wasn't going to soften his old colleague despite the pressure of his son.

Nor was his mother any help.

"Settle it with your father!"

Amanda Cobb was anything but the typical professor's wife. There was nothing tempered about her ways or her speech. She was a vigorous woman, as determined in her own way as the senator was in his. Amanda Cobb wasn't for coddling anything or anybody and she was as likely to lose her temper and let fly full blast as she was to put a clamp down on any rebellious splurge on the part of her children.

"If you think I want to see you out there playing a boy's game all your life, you're completely mistaken."

"It's not a boy's game, ma'am!"

"I don't care what kind of game it is," came

back the irritated mother. "Your father wants you to be a lawyer and a lawyer you'll be. That's that and there is no more!"

Ty's mouth grew tight, his eyes sharpened, his chin pushed out with determination. He knew where he was going and he knew that nothing was going to stop him. The will to win, the will to fight through to the very end, till victory was in his own hands, firmly and forever, was something he had inherited from his ancestors.

School was out and the diamond fever burned in him. Night was no longer for sleeping and rest. Night was for tossing in his bed, restless with dreams, restless with long debates rehearsed and repeated, restless with the desire, the need to act, to do something, to bring the whole fight to an end, a successful end.

When everybody in the house was asleep Tyrus Cobb got out of bed, dressed and quietly walked out into the streets, the deserted streets of Royston with its twenty-five hundred good souls sound in their peaceful slumber.

He moved through the lanes between the houses out into the country, in the tall grasses and along the quiet brook, among the tall trees. He might have sat down, rested against the strong trunk of an oak, taken time to let his mind rest with the stillness of the evening. But there was no rest in Tyrus Cobb and he could find no ease anywhere in Royston. His heart, his mind and every muscle of his body were already on some baseball field, swinging a bat, fielding a ball, sliding in a cloud of dust for second base.

He retraced his steps, let himself into the house, silently walked up the steps to his room and shut the door behind him. He put on his small desk light and sat down at the table.

"I can play the outfield," he wrote. "I can play the infield. I can hit and I'm fast on the bases. I would appreciate a tryout with your club."

He signed the letter and addressed it to the Augusta Club in the South Atlantic League—the Sally League as it was called more familiarly—and keeping the letter a secret from everybody, he mailed it off.

He mailed letters to every club in the Sally League and they all read pretty much the same.

"I'm a good ballplayer. I'll pay my own expenses. Let me try out for your team."

Nothing happened. For days nothing happened.

Every morning Tyrus was there to meet the mailman.

"Nothing for me?"

The mailman thumbed through the letters and cards, the folders and circulars.

"Nothing, Tyrus. Nothing."

Cobb turned his face away to hide the tears.

"Thanks," he said, and he walked off.

Generally he walked off to the local diamond. He wasn't letting up, not for a minute. Batting practice, more batting practice, fielding practice, running practice, sliding practice. Practice makes perfect. That was the rule and he held to it.

And then one day the letter came.

He steadied his hands, carefully opened the envelope. Quickly his eyes ran down the communication and he could read nothing. He walked into the house and up to his room, sat down on his bed and began all over again.

He pulled the letter out of the envelope, held the sheet of paper with the typing away from him. Slowly he read the contents. It was from Augusta, the Augusta Club, and the letter was signed by the manager of the club, Con Strouthers.

For a moment Tyrus Raymond Cobb sat on the edge of his bed stunned, then suddenly the whole thing became clear to him. His dreams were suddenly going to come true, he was going to play ball. Augusta was waiting for him. They were going to try him out. There was never any doubt in the mind of Tyrus Raymond Cobb. A tryout meant a job, a job in baseball, the baseball he wanted to play more than anything else in the world. He let out a whoop, a wild whoop of joy and leaped high in the air to spear the imaginary line drive. His hand crashed against the ceiling and he stopped suddenly in his tracks. It wasn't the pain in his hand which had stopped him. It was a voice from below.

"Tyrus!"

It was his mother.

"Tyrus!"

He walked to the door, folded the letter and hastily shoved it into his pocket.

"Yes, ma'am?"

"Was that you upstairs?"

"Yes, ma'am."

"Well I wish you'd confine your practicing to the playing field, if you have to practice at all. You nearly knocked the ceiling down on my head."

"Yes, ma'am."

Tyrus closed the door behind him, stretched out on his bed. He read the letter from Con Strouthers again. But this time he was more subdued. He had in his hands the first leg of his victory, but there was still opposition. There was Herschel Cobb still to be convinced—and he had yet to discover the weak spot in his father's armor before he could attack it, if there were a weak spot where he had encountered only the tough, indestructible wall.

He looked at the letter and his joy was tempered. He gritted his teeth and he hammered his fist into his soft pillow.

"I'm going to play for Augusta! And no one, no one is going to stop me!"

THERE were three men sitting out on the Cobb
porch in Royston the night before Tyrus Cobb was
scheduled to leave for his meeting with Con
Strouthers and the Augusta Baseball Club. There
was Herschel Cobb, cold, austere, with nothing
but contempt for the game of baseball as played in
the leagues, minor or major, and who adamantly
stuck to his resolution that his son enter the legal
profession and make a career of it. There was
Brother John Yarborough, the light from the win-
dows catching his big wave of red hair, soft spoken,
gentle, persuasive, eager for peace and good will
between the father and the son. And there was
Tyrus Raymond Cobb, his bag packed and ready,
the railroad ticket in his pocket, tight, tense,
straining at every nerve to keep the tempest
within him from bursting. This should have been
one of the happier moments in the life of the young
Cobb. Baseball was the way of life he had chosen
and the call had come to him—and from one of the

better clubs, if not the best club, in the Sally League. He should have been bursting with song and dancing in the street. Instead, he sat there on the Cobb porch listening to two men battling over him, as if the decision were not his at all, as if what others thought and felt and said were more important.

Ty Cobb was miserably unhappy. Here he was, the cockiest, the haughtiest fellow in all of Royston, and yet he was meekly and humbly putting the remainder of his whole life on the approval and the blessing of his father, a father who had never really been close to him, a father who had stood apart as his son had grown, stepping in only to discipline and make demands which found no answering chord in the heart and the mind of his willful son. It wasn't his respect for authority as such. Ty Cobb was never one to take an umpire's decision without loud and sometimes raucous protest whenever he thought he was being robbed. It was something more than the simple acceptance of the rule-of-the-elder. All through Cobb's life there was the strong urge to keep family together—the father, the mother, the children—in one happy unit. Time and again he made sacrifices to this belief in the family as an almost religious order. His whole baseball career might have been sacrificed that memorable evening on the Cobb porch, so strong was his faith in the need for harmony and good spirit in the family. The story of Tyrus Raymond Cobb, lawyer, might have equaled or even surpassed the story of Ty Cobb in baseball.

21

That evening Herschel Cobb, senator and fessor, held the wheel in the balance.

The argument began quietly, as quietly as the Georgia evening, then became heated and loud and bitter.

"As a man of God, Brother John," exclaimed the smooth-tongued senator, "you counsel me to send my son into the wickedness of bickering and brawling, drinking and carousing that they call professional baseball!"

"I urge you," answered Brother John quietly, "to cast away your prejudice. In every profession there are men, and sometimes women, who cast an ill name on the field of practice. I dare say, Senator, that there are politicians who drink and gamble and sometimes are guilty of even greater sins in the eyes of man and in the eyes of God."

"They are few and far between!" snapped the senator.

"As few and as far between as you'll find in baseball, Mr. Cobb."

"I don't like to see my son waste his life in this undignified fashion," sputtered Herschel Cobb. "He would make a good lawyer. I know he would make a good lawyer."

"He'll make a great baseball player, Mr. Cobb."

Tyrus moved uneasily in his chair.

"He's the most natural ballplayer I've ever seen," continued Big John.

"Thanks," muttered Tyrus Cobb, but there was scarcely any hope left for the approval—the blessing—he wanted from his father.

It was nearly three in the morning. In just a few hours the train he should be on would come steaming into Royston, and yet there was no sign of a break in the stone-walled opposition of the bull-headed senator.

"Sir," he broke in at last, "we've gone over this again and again, night after night, sitting exactly where we're sitting tonight. I'm afraid there's no more sense to talking anymore. We're all done talking. It's time, I think, for action."

The elder Cobb looked at his son.

"That's about as wise a thought as I've ever heard from you, Tyrus. The time has come for action. Shall we say good night?"

He began to get up from his chair but Brother John stopped him.

"I don't think you quite understand, Fessor."

The fessor sat down again.

"I think I understand perfectly."

He turned to Tyrus.

"There are a number of good law schools, son," he said. "We'll see the Judge in the morning. A letter of recommendation from him should start you right."

Ty sat speechless. His brow was all furrowed up, his eyes blazing, the shout was in his throat but nothing would come out of it.

"Mr. Cobb," began Brother John Yarborough again, "I'm afraid you've misunderstood, misunderstood completely."

"Let the boy speak!" snapped the angry senator.

Ty studied his stern, austere, relentless father, the tears coming up into his eyes.

"Sir," he began, the tears choking in his throat, "you have my respect. You have my love. I wish with all my heart that I could please you, that I could become the lawyer you want me to be. I can't. I can't." The tears were rolling down his cheeks. "I won't!" he shouted.

The senator got up from his chair slowly.

"I suppose," he said, calmly, "that that's all there is. Good night, Brother Yarborough. Good night, Tyrus."

He walked to the door, Brother John and Tyrus remaining frozen in their seats.

"I had hoped for better from my children," said the senator, turning back to the porch for a moment. "I'm sorry, Brother Yarborough, that I found no ally in you."

"You have no enemy in me," countered Brother John quickly, seizing the small opening the senator had given him. "I came here more for you than for Tyrus, Senator."

"Then I don't understand your language," answered the elder Cobb.

"Sit down," urged the brother. "Please sit down."

The senator came back to his chair, glanced at his son, whose face was buried in his open hands.

"Mr. Cobb," said Big John, "I can't know your Tyrus as well as you do. He has been in my Sunday school where I have tried to teach the respect due to elders, and it seems Tyrus came to me with that lesson learned. I have seen him on the ball field and I have never witnessed greater love given to the game. I have heard his sharp tongue and his ready wit. I have witnessed his quick temper and his fiery determination. Mr. Cobb, whether you will it or not, your son is going to play baseball. Whether you will it or not, he will make a career of it. Whether you will it or not, he will leave for Augusta. It would be better, better for you as well as for Tyrus, if he went with your blessing."

For a long moment there was a pause of silence —broken only by the occasional cry of a lonely bird in the Georgia night. For a long moment there was a heavy stillness on the Cobb porch in Royston.

"I won't ask you, Tyrus."

It was almost a hollow voice breaking the long moment of tense quiet, a broken voice, a strange note of defeat and resignation for the hardened senator from Royston.

"I know," he said. "I've known it all along."

Tyrus looked up at his father. For a quick instant there was a touch of pity in him and all his resolution wavered, teetered, was on the verge of a complete collapse.

"Sir . . ." he began.

But Herschel Cobb waved him off.

"You can go, Tyrus," the fessor said, quietly. "I give you my permission and my good wishes."

For a moment he paused, rose from his chair, and then the iron came back to his face, the sternness to his eyes, the hardness to his words.

"You can go, Tyrus," he repeated. "But once you've packed and left this house, I don't ever want to see your face again—unless you've made good. Unless you've made *good,* Tyrus!" he repeated.

"I'll make good, sir!" answered the young Cobb with fierce determination. "I'll make good, sir!"

But Herschel Cobb did not hear him. He had already left the porch and closed the door behind him.

There was one last ominous note to the evening, and it was left for Brother John to utter it.

"You'll get the job, Tyrus. Con Strouthers will like you. You'll get the job, Tyrus, but you won't hold it."

The young, eager, tortured Tyrus started to protest.

"I'll hold it. I want to hold it. I've got to hold it!"

"I know," said Big Brother John. "I know you want to hold it, but you'll be fined and fired before the season is out."

"Why?" demanded the confused Ty Cobb.

"Because you're muleheaded and you won't take orders!" slammed the brother. "Good night."

CHAPTER 4

CON STROUTHERS looked at the seventeen-year-old kid from Royston. He looked him up and down and maybe inside and out.

"Tyrus Raymond Cobb," he said. "That's quite a monicker."

He hitched up his pants, pulled the cap down over his head, hooked his thumbs inside his belt. He was hard. He was tough. And being hard and tough was almost as important to a ballplayer as being a good man with the bat, a good man in the field. There wasn't a soft spot in Con Strouthers' make-up.

His eyes burned into the youngster, skeptically, cynically.

"You haven't shaved yet, have you?"

He spat a wad of chewing tobacco out of his mouth.

"You'd better go home to Mamma," he said.

But Ty Cobb held him. Ty wasn't one to be easily frightened. While he didn't particularly enjoy the assorted phrases and remarks hurled at him, they did nothing to turn his liver. Nor did the looks in the man's eyes shrivel him up.

"You sent for me, didn't you?"

"I sent for a ballplayer."

"You sent for me," said Ty.

Con Strouthers studied the boy again. If he'd been a gentler man he would have smiled. There was something about the youngster that caught his fancy. At least, he had guts.

"Got a glove?" he asked.

"I've got a glove," answered Ty, laconically.

Strouthers stayed with the boy another minute.

"O.K.," he said, finally. "Get out there and let me see what you can do!"

Ty did all right. He did all right in the field and he did all right with the bat. Brother Yarborough had called him the most natural ballplayer he had ever seen and that was exactly what he was. With a fistful of popcorn he played out in center field, munching till a ball came his way or anywhere near him. Then like a streak he was off, in whatever the direction of the flight of the ball, and there it was, the ball in his glove, as if there were no other place in the world for the ball to be.

"You've got to chew that popcorn?" demanded Con Strouthers.

"Doesn't hurt anybody none," said Ty, and off to the bench he walked without any further comment.

Popcorn or no, he was good enough for the

rough and tough Con Strouthers to make the regular line-up.

"He's only a kid, but he's good," said the sharp Strouthers. "Seventeen," he said to himself. "I can't believe it."

Ty took to the field in the first game of the Sally League season as if he had always been there. He was excited. That's sure. When the young Cobb entered professional ball there were no dreams of glory. It was sheer joy just to handle the ball, lash out with the bat, run those bases. It was fun, just fun, that was the whole alphabet of it from *A* to *Z*. There was nothing to be tight about. It wasn't a question of making good. It was just that he liked the game, liked playing it better than anything else that he had ever thought of, read about or talked about. And there he was in center field, playing for Augusta, Georgia, and that was the most natural thing in the world to the haughtiest, cockiest kid from Royston.

Up to bat, leading off, he looked down at the pitcher studying him. And he sneered at him.

"Never mind the pose!" he shouted. "Let's see that ball!"

The pitcher rubbed the ball in the palms of his and legs. He let the ball fly and it sailed high and wide.

"Get it over!" screamed the seventeen-year-old kid.

He banged his bat down on the plate.

"Here it is!" he barked. "Let's see it!"

The pitcher rubbed the ball in the palms of his

hands. He took his windup. He was all arms and legs again. The ball came straight and fast for the plate and Ty Cobb swung—and connected.

Fast as a streak he was off and running. He rounded first, barely touched the bag, and was off for second. The hook slide, the quick tag, but he was in, and the umpire's hand shot up.

"Safe!"

"Where did *you* learn to pitch?" he yelled in to the man in the box.

"Tough!" the second baseman slapped at him.

The tempest from Georgia looked at his opposition, a man four inches taller and twenty pounds heavier than he was, even sopping wet.

"Anytime you want to find out," he said, politely, "I'll be ready to oblige you."

There was a man at first. Augusta had a four-run lead but Con Strouthers wanted that extra run. And with a man on first and just one away, there was only one way to get it. That is, according to the books there was only one way to get it.

Ty Cobb was already at the plate when Strouthers called him back.

"Bunt!" he said, curtly.

"Why?" asked the irascible Cobb.

"Bunt!" ordered Strouthers.

Ty just looked at him and walked back to the batting box.

Anybody knew why the bunt was the strategy. A man on second can be brought home with a single. It takes at least two singles to bring a man from first.

But that wasn't the way Ty figured it.

He let the first pitch sail by. It was wide and low.

"Ball!" called the umpire.

The coach at third signaled the bunt again.

Ty saw it, nodded his head.

The second pitch came inside and high. Ty Cobb watched it go by, saw the quick peg to first, the quick tag, just too late by an eyelash.

The coach at third almost yelled it this time.

"Bunt!"

Ty nodded again.

This time the pitch came where Tyrus liked it and he lashed out with his bat and the bat met the ball squarely. Like a rising rocket it sailed, gaining height in its flight, a flight that did not end till the ball had sailed clearly out of the park.

Tyrus Cobb was all smiles circling the bases. It was his first home run in professional ball. He was mighty pleased with himself.

But Con Strouthers wasn't pleased.

"I told you to bunt!" he snapped.

"I hit a home run, didn't I?" Tyrus snapped.

"I told you to bunt!" barked the irate manager.

"I got the man around!" shouted the angry youngster.

"And you've got yourself out!" slammed the fiery Strouthers. "You take orders on this ball club! You don't give them!"

If the meaning wasn't clear to the rookie then, it became clear enough the next afternoon.

For reasons best known to Strouthers, Ty was in

center field for the second game. Probably there was no one to replace him at the moment, or maybe the blunt manager wanted twenty-four hours to think it over. Whatever the case, after that second game for Augusta, Tyrus Raymond Cobb was given his walking papers—and as quickly as he had gotten into professional ball he was out.

Brother John Yarborough had been prophetic.

"You'll be fired before the season is out, because you're muleheaded and you won't take orders."

It had been a mighty short first season for Tyrus and he was a pretty puzzled and fretting youngster, writing the news back home.

What would his father say now? How was he going to face him?

The answer came back faster than he had expected. But it gave him no solace, no comfort. On the contrary.

DON'T COME BACK A FAILURE.

It was a five-word telegram and it was signed by Herschel Cobb.

"Don't come back a failure!"

Ty Cobb clenched the wire in his hand, tossed it into a corner, paced his room, stopped where the crumpled telegram had landed. He picked it up again, spread it out before him.

"Failure! Failure!"

The word rang in his ears.

"Never!" he shouted. "Never!"

And the tears shot up into his eyes, but they were not tears of pity, not tears of regret and fear; they were tears of anger and resolution, tears of fight and determination. They were Ty Cobb tears, the kind of tears which would lift him head and shoulders into the upper strata of baseball history and baseball fame.

CHAPTER 5

THERE was another bit of communication the seventeen-year-old Tyrus Cobb received while he was still hanging around in Augusta, after he had been slapped down by the toughened manager of the Augusta Baseball Club, Con Strouthers. It wasn't a telegram and the words were not so curt, but the message was no sweeter. If Con Strouthers' thumbing him out of the Augusta ball park was strike one, and the wire from his father was strike two, then this third note—the letter from Royston —was strike three.

There was a girl in Royston, a pretty girl, and Tyrus had known her for as long as he could remember. More than that, Tyrus had been in love with her and the girl had been in love with him.

"You won't mind being a ballplayer's wife?" he had asked her.

They had been sitting at the edge of a small stream on the outskirts of the town, talking about life the way seventeen-year-old kids talk about life, talking about love the way seventeen-year-old kids talk about love.

"You're not proposing?" said the girl, answering the question Tyrus had put to her with a query of her own.

Ty tossed a pebble into the water.

"I don't have to propose, do I?"

"No," said the girl, simply.

"We'll be traveling in the summertime," said Tyrus, after a minute, "but then we can be home together all winter."

"That shouldn't be too hard," corroborated the young sweetheart.

"As a matter of fact," added Tyrus, "we won't ever be far from home, even in the summertime. It won't be a big home at first," he explained. He never apologized. "But it will grow," he asserted.

And the pretty little girl in Royston blushed and nodded her head solemnly in agreement.

But now there was the letter and the dreams of two seventeen-year-old kids lay smashed and scattered on it.

"It's all over, Tyrus," she had written. "There is nothing I can do. Both my mother and my father are completely against it. They say that they won't let a man who plays baseball for money enter their parlor. They certainly won't let a man who plays baseball for money see their daughter. They mean me, Tyrus, and maybe they are right. Maybe it would be better if you forgot. Maybe it would be better if we both forgot. This is the last time I'm writing to you. Good luck, Tyrus, and good-by."

Perhaps it was only puppy love; perhaps it was more. But whatever kind of love it is, a seventeen-year-old heart can break as easily and as quickly as the hearts of people much older. It very easily could have been strike three for the young fellow, who had just pushed out on his own despite every kind of opposition. He could have been broken right then and there. But not Ty Cobb.

He folded the letter carefully, put it back in its envelope. Slowly his face grew tighter, his eyes harder. He sat down to write his answer.

"Meet me here in Augusta. I don't care what anyone thinks and I don't want you to care. I'll be waiting for you here at the. . . ."

His pen trailed off. For a moment his mind wandered back to Royston, the quiet of the town, the peacefulness of the twenty-five hundred people who lived in it. Then he remembered the telegram his father had sent him and the serenity of his mood changed. He recalled Con Strouthers' bouncing him off the first professional team he had made —he recalled the home run he had hit, the home run which had caused his first setback. And suddenly he was on his feet, pacing the room, banging his fist into the palm of his hand. No one was going to make him turn back. No one was going to dictate the way of life he was going to lead. If no one was behind him he would do it alone, but he would do it, he would do it.

He picked up the letter he had started, glanced at it, then threw it away. He took the letter from

36

the girl in Royston, scanned it once. For a moment his face softened, then slowly his fist closed around the missive of rejection. Nothing would stop him! Nothing and nobody! His hand opened. He straightened out the crumpled letter and slowly, deliberately, tore it into shreds. Tyrus Raymond Cobb was pledged to the game, the game of baseball.

There was a spot for him on the Anniston Baseball Club in the Southeastern League—and he got it.

"This club in Alabama is a pretty good outfit," he wrote home. "Watch me go."

And go he did. He played in twenty-two games for the Anniston Club, hit a magnificent .370 and stole six bases. He was a find for the Anniston Association at fifty dollars a month. He was a find for any club playing ball.

That was exactly what he wrote in a letter to the sports editor of the Atlanta *Journal*. The editor was Grantland Rice, one of the most beloved and respected men in the sports world.

"You want to see this kid in action," he wrote. "He handles his bat like a veteran and he covers the field like a major league ballplayer."

He wrote about Ty Cobb but didn't sign it Ty Cobb. It was as if he were just an interested spectator and had seen a boy who ought to get some notice.

A ballplayer leading the league in batting, any league, deserves and gets notice. Ty Cobb's notices about himself didn't all land in the wastepaper basket, and people in Augusta began to ask, "How come this kid was dropped? What's the matter with Con Strouthers? How come he wasn't good enough for Augusta and he's burning up the league for Anniston? How come Con Strouthers?"

Con Strouthers wasn't in a position to answer that for very long. The Augusta Club fired him and George Leidy was now managing the team. Leidy played the outfield for the Sally League Club, and while there hadn't been time for him to get to know the seventeen-year-old boy from Royston in his short stay with the team he had taken good note of his natural ability on the diamond.

In short order, Tyrus Cobb was back with Augusta where the outfielder-manager George Leidy was to play a most important role in shaping the career of the Royston wildcat.

It wasn't in the techniques of the game that Leidy was most helpful. Ty was out there all the time, practicing his swing at the bat, changing his stance, experimenting all the while. No one in baseball knows—or has known—as much about the art of batting as the Peach from Georgia. And no one has ever known anything more about the art of running bases or stealing them. No one gave these elements of baseball greater study or more concentrated hours of sheer hard work for perfection. It wasn't in the finer points of baseball that George Leidy instructed the youngster, it was in the world of possibilities that lay before him if he regarded the game as a steppingstone or an open door.

"They pay big money in the big leagues, Tyrus," said Leidy.

"How much?"

"More than you can count."

"That would have to be a whole lot."

"It is a whole lot."

"Then I'll play for the big leagues."

"You'll have to give up eating popcorn in the field then," said George Leidy.

"But I like eating popcorn," protested the kid.

"Then eat it on the bench. Eat in bed. You can't give the game everything if half your hands are on popcorn."

Tyrus looked at the older man.

"Tell me more."

And George Leidy told him more. He told him of the big cities where the major-leaguers played. He drew word-pictures of the huge crowds that filled the stadiums. He painted word pictures of the excitement, the tremendous heartbeat of the fight for the pennant, the battle for the World's Championship in the tense and dramatic World Series.

The boy listened, drank it all in. Baseball, he was discovering, was more than just fun. It was the key to a golden future, the kind of future his father had wanted of him, demanded of him. George Leidy's words took effect. The boy from Royston continued to spend his hours in the batting cage and the sliding pits. But now it was not only the perfection of the game he was after, it was all the rewards that the game offered.

It was hard for him to give up chewing popcorn in the outfield, but when a ball went by him and spoiled a shutout for Eddie Cicotte—the man who was to become one of the greatest pitchers in baseball, only to throw away his career in the famous, or infamous, Black Sox scandal—when that ball went by Ty Cobb, the terror of Royston banged his glove to the ground and emptied his pockets of the accursed popcorn, never to eat it again. That is, never to eat it again while he was playing the game in the outfield.

But that was early in 1905, and 1905 was one of the more dramatic years in the dramatic life of Tyrus Raymond Cobb.

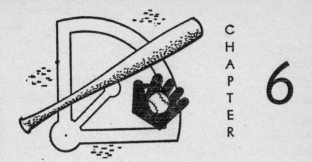

DURING spring training in 1905 the Detroit Tigers got their first good look at Tyrus Cobb. The club was training in Augusta and played a number of games with the Sally League team. It was a good team, too. Cicotte was pitching for the minor-leaguers at the time, and so was Nap Rucker, the same Nap Rucker who was to come up with the Brooklyn Superbas, Trolley-car Dodgers or just Dodgers—as they were called by those who didn't call them "Them Bums." Nap Rucker became one of the best southpaw flingers the game has ever known and he was good enough in Georgia to impress the mighty Detroit Tigers.

Bill Yawkey, uncle of Tom Yawkey who owns the Boston Red Sox, was president and owner of the Tigers at that time, Frank Navin was secretary-treasurer—two of baseball's greatest men-behind-the-scenes. Wild Bill Donovan was pitching for them. Bill Armour, who had learned his baseball under Ed Barrow of New York Yankee fame, was managing the club. The funnyman in baseball, good-nature Germany Schaefer was playing second. It was a team that was to finish third in the American League race that year. Still, the Augusta squad was no push-over and the Tigers treated them with the full respect due them.

It was different with Tyrus Raymond Cobb.

"That's just about the craziest fielding I've ever seen," said George Mullin, star Detroit pitcher. "That kid's all over the lot."

"Someone ought to tell him he's playing just center field," said another bemused big-leaguer, "not right field, left field, center field and second base."

"He's crazy on the bases," said Wild Bill Donovan. "Doesn't know when to stop. He'll run himself sick, he will."

"Just crazy," said Germany Schaefer, and the funnyman buried a laugh in his hands. "Just crazy. That's all."

It isn't surprising that Ty Cobb didn't impress the Tiger squad as a potentially great ballplayer. He was wild in the field and wilder on the base paths. He was a natural ballplayer and he had given himself completely to developing himself in it. Still, there were things about the game he had to learn—for example, that there's no sense chasing a ball that is heading far beyond the possible reach of a baseball mitt, for the roof of an apartment house a couple of streets outside the park. There's very little sense making a dash for third base when the third baseman has the ball in his hand, waiting

42

for you. But Ty Cobb rarely subscribed to this philosophy of the game. He was always in there—trying for the impossible catch, trying for that almost impossible base. Almost impossible because Ty Cobb was later to take bases which no one else would ever dream of taking.

Baseball, in 1905, was not the big-power game it is today. It wasn't often that the home run ball decided the score. One run was a big run in those days, even in the early innings, and good base running was the essence of that one run. Daring base running was perhaps the greatest thing in baseball in those days when the long ball was still a dream incubating in the minds of some few big-leaguers.

There was no question that Ty Cobb's base running was daring those afternoons which saw the Tigers playing against the Georgia team. But it was more startling than daring, and it amused more than it impressed.

"Crazy," said Germany Schaefer, "just crazy."

However, late in the season of that year the Detroit Tigers, battling for third place in their league, ran into a series of injuries which threatened their hopes and aspirations. Bill Armour, managing the team, sent out a call for help, and the help he expected was to come from the South Atlantic League.

Bill Armour had been reading the reports of the games, following the batting averages and other details of the sport as it was being played in the Sally League. And one name had struck him and stayed with him. That kid with Augusta, the kid who didn't know he was playing just center field, not the whole diamond, the kid who didn't know when he didn't have a chance for that extra base, the kid who went sliding into a bag, stealing it, as if his whole life depended on it. The name of the kid was Ty Cobb and he was leading his league in batting at the cute clip of .326—one hundred and thirty-four hits in four hundred and eleven times at bat. Besides, he had forty stolen bases to his credit, forty stolen bases in one hundred and four games.

"That's better than one in every three games," calculated Armour quickly.

Heinie Youngman, Detroit scout, looked at his boss.

"Shall I go take a look?"

"Go take a look," said Bill Armour. "Maybe he's the guy we need."

Youngman went, but he couldn't see Cobb.

"Spiked," said Tyrus, showing him his bruised thumb.

"That's a pretty good record you're piling up for yourself," said Heinie.

"Just the beginning," said Tyrus who was never too modest about the truth.

Heinie Youngman might have waited around for that spiked thumb to heal. He might have wired back to Detroit that the hellion out of Royston was out of the line-up. He did neither. He laid seven hundred and fifty dollars on the line and Tyrus Raymond Cobb became the property of the Detroit Ball Club. That seven hundred and fifty dollars was about the best investment a ball club ever made, and the "crazy kid," the madcap from Georgia, didn't take too long to pay off dividends for the hard-pressed Tigers.

The date was August 30, 1905, the scene Bennett Field in Detroit. The Tigers were entertaining the New York Highlanders. Pitching for the New Yorkers was that all-time great, the man with the spitball, the brilliant Jack Chesbro. In the box for the Detroiters was the good George Mullin. This was the date, the place and the setting when Ty Cobb walked into his first major league line-up. This was the setting for Ty Cobb's debut in the big time. He was still only a kid and he might very well have had a few jitters, finding himself suddenly in the rarefied atmosphere of major league ball. A look at the big boys—the big names of the sport —is sometimes enough to freeze the blood of a young rookie, paralyze every muscle in him, fix him in his tracks like a rock of salt. But not Ty Cobb. Instinctively he sensed hostility, the hostility which was the rule in those earlier days of baseball toward any youngster breaking into the game to take away some old-timer's place in the batting order, some old-timer's place in the field. Instinctively he knew that he wasn't welcome in center field or at the plate. He made a mental note of it. At the moment there was other business at hand and he looked neither at Sam Crawford, who was playing right field, nor at McIntyre who was playing left field, nor at anybody else. He just put on his glove and walked out into the sun—and into glory.

The line-up of the Tigers that memorable afternoon was Matty McIntyre in left field and leading off, Lindsay at first base, Germany Schaefer at second, Sam Crawford in right field, and Tyrus Raymond Cobb in center field and batting fifth. Coughlin was at third, O'Leary at short, Drill behind the bat and, pitching, the Brilliant George Mullin.

For the up-and-coming New York Highlanders it was Conroy at first, Keeler in right field, Elberfeld at short, Williams at second, Yaeger at the hot corner, Hahn covering center field, Delahanty in left, McGuire catching and that all-time great, Jack Chesbro, pitching.

Chesbro was a spitball pitcher, the best spitter, perhaps, in the business. In 1904 he had turned in forty-one victories for the Highlanders. Today a twenty-game winner is feted and sung all over the place, and rightly so, but in 1904 Jack Chesbro was twice twenty a winner—and more. It will be a very long time before the big leagues produce a pitcher who will take that many games in a single season, if ever again.

It was against this same master, this same Jack Chesbro, that Ty Cobb made his debut at the plate in the big time.

McIntyre, with all due respect for the pitcher's greatness, greeted him with a two-bagger. Lindsay promptly sent him home with a solid single. Not an auspicious beginning for the great spitter, but

46

he settled down and there were two out when the busher from Augusta stepped up to the plate.

If Ty Cobb had been jittery coming up for his first lick in the majors it would have been understandable, but there was nothing jittery about the eighteen-year-old kid. He was cocky, self-assured and determined. He tapped the plate with his bat, looked out to the mound and swung his bat menacingly at the pitcher.

Chesbro looked back at second where Lindsay, pushed up by one of the deep infield outs, stood waiting to be moved on. The pitcher toed the rubber and sent a fast one across the plate. Ty swung but he didn't get it.

"Strike one!"

Chesbro glanced back to second, fired again to the plate. Cobb watched it go by.

"Strike two!" bawled the umpire.

Chesbro didn't bother looking back to second. He wound up, snapped the ball in and the young Georgian met it—hard. The pellet shot on a line past the center fielder, and Tyrus Raymond Cobb raced to first, turned and sped toward second, slid into the dust and made it. Lindsay had scored, Ty Cobb had made his first hit in the major leagues— his first double—and batted in his first run. It was a suitable debut for the Georgia Peach.

C
H
A
P
T
E
R

7

TY COBB moved into the major leagues in 1905. This was also the year that the boy from Royston suffered the first major tragedy in his young life. Just before he left Augusta for Detroit he was suddenly called from the playing field and informed that he was wanted at home at once. Herschel Cobb, the stern, the austere, the cold and driving father of the kid ballplayer would send him no more wires, would no longer demand of his son that he follow this or that profession, could no longer shout, "Don't come home a failure."

The elder Cobb had quietly and unobtrusively followed the story of his rebellious son as it developed with the Anniston Club, with the Augusta Club. He had, in his own peculiar way, been proud of the boy. It wasn't in the senator to sing the praises of his family, to show outwardly his love for it, but every once in a while he let slip his approval of his son's progress. Not once, however, did he find words to praise the younger Cobb to his face, or even in a sealed letter. And now it was too late.

Under circumstances which were clouded, in an atmosphere of enigma and cloaked in mystery, Herschel Cobb, the fessor, the senator from Royston, Georgia, was shot and killed. He never saw his son play in the big leagues. He never read of the acclaim which came to his name. Before the dream of his first-born had flowered into one of the greatest careers, if not *the* greatest career on the diamond, Herschel Cobb was dead.

"Don't come home a failure!"

Tyrus Cobb didn't weep. He was silent, his face white and drawn, tension in his creased forehead, strain in his eyes. He remembered what his father might have been to him. He remembered what his father was. Respect was there. He wished that love was there, too.

"Don't come home a failure!"

The words kept repeating themselves in his ears, in his heart. This was what his father had meant to him. This was everything his father had meant to him.

"Don't come home a failure!"

He remembered it as he sat on the Tiger bench, a boy of eighteen among men many years older, men who were perhaps much wiser than he, certainly men with more knowledge of the ways of the world than the mere youngster fresh from Georgia.

It was bad enough that he was a rookie and that he had been put into the line-up without the customary couple of years spent warming the bench. It was that southern drawl, the gentility of the southern manners and the fact that he had come up north from under the Mason-Dixon line that made matters even worse.

"You-all go get you-all-self a glove," they mimicked, "and go chase you-all a few flies, busher!"

The "busher" was uttered with undisguised and unmitigated venom.

"What's the matter, you old codgers?" came back the pugnacious Cobb, forgetting the niceties taught at home. "You too broken down to crawl out there in the sun?"

Ty Cobb wasn't one to take any kind of punishment lying down.

"Better not swing too hard. The wood in your arms will be splintering all over the field."

A rookie was supposed to take it, not give it. Ty Cobb didn't know the rules. He dished it out as fast as it was given—and that didn't make him any dearer or nearer to his teammates. On the contrary, the harder he fought back the more vicious was the attack on the boy.

They pushed him out of the batter's cage and Ty, hat in hand, went up to Bill Armour to ask whether he couldn't take his turn hitting them out.

There was no hint of complaint in his voice, no hint of the rough treatment he was getting from the other boys.

"I'd like to sharpen up a bit at the plate, Mr. Armour. Is it all right if I take a couple of swings?"

Maybe Bill Armour knew what was happening and maybe he didn't.

"Go ahead, boy," he said. "Go ahead."

But when Ty picked up his bat it wasn't just one solid piece of wood, it was two useless hunks of timber. One of the more playful Bengals had sawed the thing in two.

Ty just looked around him at the cold, expressionless faces of his teammates, dropped the lumber and walked off.

"Don't come home a failure! Don't come home a failure!"

The words kept repeating, repeating, repeating.

Baseball had its great men in 1905, but the spirit you find in baseball today was not there. John McGraw was the Little Napoleon running his New York Giants with an iron hand, and winning pennants with them. The screwball Rube Waddell was winning twenty-seven games for Connie Mack and the Philadelphia Athletics. There was Nap Lajoie with the Cleveland Indians and the immortal Hans Wagner playing at third base for the Pittsburgh Pirates. Nick Altrock, who with Al Schacht was later to become the Clown Prince of Baseball, was playing a great game for Chicago. The great Tinkers to Evers to Chance infield combination of the Chicago Cubs was in operation and Scanlan was pitching great ball for the Brooklyn Superbas. There was Iron-man Joe McGinty and—almost an anomaly in the hurly-burly, hard-as-nails and hotter-than-fire days of baseball—the gentle, college-bred Christy Mathewson, as great a name as base-ball has ever boasted.

But the fine and sportsmanlike practice of picking up the rookie, showing him the finer points of fielding, showing him the finer points of hitting, just showing him that he was welcome and "here's hoping you can make it" was not there. When Ty Cobb broke into the game it was every man for himself. If the fledgling couldn't get off the ground and learn how to fly for himself, that was the fledgling's business. And the fewer rookies, the better chance for the veteran to hold onto his job and to stick on the clubs's payroll.

"Out of the way, busher!"

"Why don't you-all go back to Georgia?"

"What have you-all got there, boy? That's my soup you're drinking."

A shove of the plate and the soup was in the young Cobb's lap.

"I don't like anybody drinking my soup."

"And nobody's going to spill soup in my lap and get away with it!" flared the tyro from Georgia.

But there were ten hands on him before he could get started and the only thing for him to do was to get up and leave the table.

By the end of his first season with Detroit, or part of it, Ty Cobb had played in forty-one games, gotten thirty-six hits, stolen a couple of bases and made a personal enemy of every other man on the squad.

"You're in my way, busher."

"Carry my glove, boy."

"You're in the North, you-all, rookie, not in you-all magnolias."

And the more he got the more he gave.

"Why don't you get yourself a crutch, you old bag!"

"They've got blind men can see a ball faster than you old mules!"

"Why don't you let someone who can play show you? I was better in my knee pants than you'll ever be, you loud-mouthed croaker!"

He could have been discouraged, he might have been beaten, if he hadn't been Ty Cobb. Instead the venom grew in him, his hatred grew in him, and his determination to show up all his vicious teammates made him drive harder for the place he always insisted was his.

"First place," he said. "That's where I belong. First place. It belongs to me."

Nap Rucker, that all-time great, told the story again and again.

It was when they were both playing ball for Augusta. Nap had strolled into the bathroom before the rest of the boys had come off the field. He was taking his peaceful shower when the thunder descended. At least, that's what it sounded like, the terrible banging on the door.

"Who's in there?"

It was angry and demanding.

"Me! What do you want?"

"Get out! Get out of there!"

"What for?"

"Get out!"

"Says you!"

"Says I!"

It was one of those running, endless battles that generally end with fists flying, and Nap Rucker, after he had taken his own sweet time, finally opened the door of the bathroom and was ready to meet whatever the irate Cobb was going to throw at him.

For a moment they glared at each other.

"What's all the yelling about?" asked Rucker, sharply.

"I'm in that bathroom first!" snapped the fist-clenched Cobb.

"Since when?" said Nap, not giving an inch.

"I'm always first!" shot the blazing younster, and Nap Rucker just stared at him.

"First place belongs to me!" exclaimed the bellicose kid from Royston. "Don't you forget it!"

Nap Rucker was still staring as the boy slammed the door behind him, but he never forgot those sharp-tempered, vehemently spit words: "First place belongs to me."

It was first place he struggled for against the whole of the Detroit Club. Things came to a head in the spring of the Georgian's second season with the Tigers, early in 1906.

Ty took an unmerciful beating from his hard-boiled teammates in his 1905 season with the Tigers. And there was no sign of a letup when the 1906 training sessions of the Detroit Bengals got under way in Georgia.

Tyrus Raymond Cobb was the guy nobody liked, the rookie who wouldn't knuckle under to the kind of hazing which was pretty generally accepted practice in the baseball of those rough-and-ready days of the sport. Every kind of abuse was heaped on his young head, every kind of indignity was visited on him. They tied his clothes up in knots; they tossed them under the running shower; they roughed him out of the batter's cage and kicked his suitcase open and down a flight of stairs. Off the field or on the field they did everything to destroy the morale of the kid from Georgia, destroy his confidence, break down his spirit. But they didn't succeed. The only thing they accomplished was to help develop an angry, bitter youngster, an angry and bitter ballplayer, an angry and bitter loner.

There wasn't a man on the club young Ty Cobb would walk off with, not a man on the club he could talk to. He ate alone, drank alone, even found a room for himself far from the hotels where the club would congregate to eat and drink and talk baseball. When the club traveled, Ty Cobb moved himself as far away from his teammates as possible.

But being the loner wasn't the answer to the wrath built up in the hot-tempered Georgian. The anger smoldered in him and it had to have some outlet before he was entirely consumed by it, so he settled on Charlie (Dutch) Schmidt. Charlie Schmidt was the biggest, the heaviest, the strongest man on the Detroit squad.

Dutch Schmidt was one of the milder men in baseball at the time. Like a lot of big men, it may have been fear of his own strength that kept him so easygoing, so gentle, so really good natured. Baseball has had its share of powerful men, but there never was a man stronger than Dutch. He could hammer nails into wood with his bare fists. He could bend a rod of iron with his bare hands. He had been good enough to step into the ring with the great Jack Johnson who, just two years later, knocked out Tommy Burns for the heavyweight championship of the world. He was built to order for the tempestuous, fearless, pugnacious Tyrus Cobb, who would tackle nothing but the best, no one but the strongest, no one but the most powerful to demonstrate his contempt and scorn for the browbeating and the bullying his teammates were heaping on him.

Charlie Schmidt stretched himself out on the clubhouse floor and defied the while team to pick him up.

"Go on! Try it! You can't! You can't pick me up from the floor!"

The whole squad set itself to the impossible task, the whole team, that is, with the exception of Ty Cobb.

Ty Cobb took one look at the prostrate figure and stepped down on his hand—hard.

It didn't take more than half a second for half of the Detroit squad to shove off the brash youngster.

"I was just trying to get him up from the floor," sneered the boy they couldn't intimidate.

"That's all right," said Dutch. "He didn't get me up, did he?"

The ring around Ty Cobb was menacing. It wouldn't have taken much to set the fists flying.

"Come on!" yelled Dutch. "I'm not going to lie here all night! Pick me up!"

Reluctantly the ring broke up. Dutch Schmidt, for the time being, had saved the boy from Georgia from a pretty bad mauling.

That didn't do anything to ease the madcat from Royston. He despised the whole squad. Maybe he despised Dutch Schmidt more than the rest, because he was the strongest, burliest, most powerful of the lot.

"Why don't you get some of that fat off you?" he shouted at him when the Dutchman got up to bat.

"Why don't you get yourself a tin cup and a batch of pencils?" he bawled at him, whenever the easygoing Charlie Schmidt missed one at the plate.

"Learn how to throw, you squarehead," he trumpeted across the field when the catcher missed a man going down to second in a swirl of dust.

Every last chance he got—and there were chances he invented—Ty Cobb did his utmost to humiliate the gentle Dutch. Actually, it was every man on the Detroit squad that he wanted to humiliate.

Once he doused the catcher with water. Another time he peppered his soup with a handful of the hot stuff. Every trick played on the Royston kid, the boy played on Dutch Schmidt. Dutch Schmidt had become the symbol of the Tiger and Ty Cobb was venting all his spleen on him.

The good-natured Dutch took it. He took it for a long time. But no man, however gentle, can take it forever. He knew that sooner or later he was going to lose control, that sooner or later he was going to forget himself. Dutch Schmidt began to avoid the demon from Georgia.

Whenever Ty came in his direction he walked away. Whenever he spotted the kid he turned away. He didn't want to get embroiled and for a long while he was a master at side-stepping the final showdown.

Ty Cobb should have let well enough alone, but he never knew how to stop short of any goal. The more Dutch avoided him, the more he sought him out.

One day he caught up. Tyrus took the first swing —and that was all. Charlie Schmidt was too much for him. He gave Ty Cobb one of the most unmerciful whippings he ever suffered in all his life. The only whipping that might have compared with it was the return match Ty Cobb clamored for and got.

Dutch might have pulled his punches in those two meetings, but not much. The eighteen-year-old kid from Georgia was battered from pillar to post, while the Detroit Club looked on, shouting encouragement to Charlie, enjoying the terrific lacing the cocky kid from under the Mason-Dixon line was taking.

"Let him have it, Dutch!"

"Give it to him, boy!"

"Attaboy, Charlie!"

Only Charlie didn't like it.

He looked at the kid's face, the cut lip, the swollen nose.

"Take him away!" he yelled. "Take him away!"

But no one took him away and the kid kept coming in for more.

A right to the jaw, a left to the jaw and the kid went down.

"Stop him!" pleaded Charlie.

"Yellow!" spit Ty Cobb, and he was up on his feet again, swinging away at the stone wall facing him. The Cobb kid, the Cobb man, for that matter, never knew what it was to quit.

It was only when the kid was helpless on his feet that the Tiger squad finally intervened to stop the one-sided melee before it ended in murder. There was no love for the boy, and there certainly was no pity. Even after this display of sheer guts on the part of the youngster, there was no change in their attitude toward the boy from Georgia. Charlie Schmidt was their man and the Royston kid a haughty, cocky, pugnacious scrapper who didn't know enough to call it enough when he was licked.

It was his pride and his bellicose refusal to accept anything that was handed to him that turned Cobb into the man who walked alone, ate alone, lived alone. He was a loner, all right, a fighting loner, who battled singlehanded to his final and indisputable victory against all odds in the game he had chosen. Whatever the squad thought of him, however, the whole club mistreated, badgered, heckled and attempted to destroy him, it was the final figures in the record books against which they had to fight at last, and those figures were something no one could belittle—figures which made every one of his teammates stop to take a second look, figures which had his name in headlines in every sport sheet in the country.

For all the ill will and ill practice which would have broken any other tenderfoot, Ty Cobb got himself one hundred and twelve hits in his first full season at Detroit—thirteen doubles, seven triples and a home run in the ninety-seven games he played for the team. He stole twenty-three bases to boot. He wasn't the league's leading hitter that year but he was right up there with the best of them with a tremendous first-year batting average of .320. He wasn't the league's best stealer that year but twenty-three stolen bases in ninety-seven games was still a mark to shoot at. There was no question about the value of Ty Cobb to his team. Detroit would have yelled itself hoarse in protest had there been any talk of trading the eighteen-year-old out of the town. The boy from Georgia had made good and even his bitterest rivals and worst tormentors had to admit it.

There were some—not many but some—who already had an inkling of the greatness of the young ballplayer. But even these men of foresight and understanding could not begin to guess at his tremendous potential.

That first full year of Ty Cobb's with the Detroit Club wasn't a particularly auspicious year. As a matter of fact they slipped from their third-place standing in 1906 to the second division and sixth in the American League standings. The one saving gesture of the entire season was perhaps the three-game series with the New York Highlanders who had come fresh from taking a crucial series from the White Sox and seemed to have the junior circuit flag all sewn up. All that the hapless Tigers did against the high-flying New Yorkers was to sweep the floor with them three times running, and drop them out of the Number One slot in the league. It was a blow from which the Highlanders couldn't recover and the White Sox from the Windy City

—the Hitless Wonders of 1906—went on to cop the pennant and the World Series, too.

But if 1906 was a disappointing year for the Tiger squad, 1907 was to tell a different story, and it was in 1907 that Cobb was to don the magnificent mantle of baseball glory, a glory that grew and developed with the years into one of the richest, if not *the* richest story in baseball.

CHAPTER 9

THE average big-leaguer, if he isn't winning his ten and fifteen games a season tossing them across the plate, is the extraordinary ball handler, the extraordinary batsman. Even your weakest man in the line-up must be immeasurably superior to the general run of ballplayers to get himself a job with any of the major league teams, even the teams which end up the year in the cellars of their divisions. Sometimes the good fans lose sight of this little fact, especially when their home teams are going nowhere in particular. The club managers, however, and the men up in the front offices never forget it. Ty Cobb certainly wasn't the most popular man with the Detroit Tigers. It isn't the best thing for a team to be split with animosities, ill tempers and just plain fights. Players have been traded overnight for less, and there might have been plenty of reasons to ship the fiery Georgian off to some other club, but Detroit wasn't trading a kid who batted .320 in his first full season with the club. He had already shown too much power to be swapped lightly with any of the seven other teams in the league. Even at that, Clark Griffith, then running the New York Club, came within an ace of landing the youngster in a trade with Detroit. It was a deal he muffed because at that time he thought the Tigers were asking too much.

In 1907 the great "Ee-yah" man came to manage the Tigers—enthusiastic, dynamic, brilliant Hugh Jennings. Jennings had played shortstop for the legendary Baltimore Orioles, along with the legendary John McGraw and Uncle Wilbert Robinson. The Orioles had been by far the roughest, toughest, rowdiest, fightingest aggregation of baseball players in the story of the game. John McGraw had brought all that fight and spirit with him to the New York Giants, and it had paid off in pennant after pennant in the older circuit. Hugh Jennings, despite his "Ee-yah," was considerably more gentle than the Little Napoleon of the Polo Grounds, less likely to fly off the handle, less likely to get his fists up and going. He was a friendlier fellow, too, and there wasn't much of the iron hand and the iron fist in his handling of players. But he could kick up a lot of dust and tear up the garden around third base—and the old spirit of the old Orioles was unmistakably there. One of the unforgettable pictures in baseball is the figure of Hugh Jennings, raising his leg, clenching his fist and letting loose with that great cry of his—"Ee-yah!"

Ee-yah had been a terrific shortstop in his playing days. With the Baltimore teams which had won pennants in 1894, 1895, and 1896, he had hit at .332, .386 and .397. He had been fast on the bases, too, stealing sixty of them in 1895 and seventy-two in 1896. If he didn't teach Ty Cobb anything about batting and base-stealing, he certainly must have inspired him. Actually, there wasn't too much contact between the two men. The Georgian had already set the pattern of his life in the baseball world. He trusted the friendship of no man on the club, or any other club, and he carried on whatever private life he lived away from any one of his inimical teammates. Even if a Tiger had tried to make amends for past performances, the Georgia Peach would have turned a deaf ear and walked off. Not that anybody tried to make amends and not that Hugh Jennings tried too hard to be friendly. Hugh Jennings just stuck the twenty-year-old kid into the line-up regularly and out into the outfield regularly, and the kid did his stuff. He did it so well that the Detroit Tigers, right from the beginning of the season, moved out of the second division and into contention for the American League flag.

As a matter of fact, that 1907 race was one of the hottest in the junior circuit's history. Four teams battled for top honors—Chicago, the same Hitless Wonders who had won the World Championship in 1906, the Cleveland Club, then known as the Naps, Connie Mack's Philadelphia Athletics and the lowly Detroit Tigers. No one really took the Bengals too seriously. After all, they were practically the same club which had finished so miserably the year before. Manager Jennings had put some life into them, some spirit, and that Ty Cobb was playing sensational ball, but how long could the spirit last, how far could it carry them—and how much longer could the twenty-year-old kid continue to bat as if he owned every pitcher in the league?

The White Sox were up there in first most of the way, but the other three clubs were pretty hot on their tails. First it was Cleveland who shoved them out for a while, then Connie Mack's men, then the Naps again. The Tigers were chewing away all the while, first in the third slot, then the fourth, then back again to third. All June and most of July they were a pesky squad which couldn't recognize it had no right being up there in the first division. At least that was the way the three other leading teams considered them. Not Hugh Jennings, not Ty Cobb, not the high-riding Bengals from Detroit.

Toward the end of July the picture changed, not for the belligerent Tigers, but for the rest of the boys who played ball in the American League. On the twenty-fifth of that hot summer month the Bengals from Detroit shoved the Cleveland Naps into third place in the race and took over the exalted position of runner-up to the league leaders. The Tigers weren't just showing an early season flash, they were really in the race with a pugnacious will to get to the top rung. The rest of the American-Leaguers sat up and took notice, and none too soon. Eight days later the up-and-coming city of

66

the automobile went wild with a fever completely new to that growing town—pennant fever. For
the first time in its history, Detroit was in first
place. The Tigers hit the front page of every newspaper. For the first time, the Detroit Tigers were
up in front, in the very front of the big race for
the league's bunting, and the front office had to
restrain itself from printing its World Series tickets.

Of course no one wins the pennant as early as
August 2—the season was still young—but the spirit was there and the fight was there, and with Cobb
batting up in the .350's there was more than an
outside chance that the Bengals would cop the
banner.

The real class team in the league in 1907 was
the Philadelphia Athletics. Connie Mack had one of
the most sensational pitching staffs in the game's
story. He had the great Indian Chief Bender,
Eddie Plank, Jack Coombs and the immortal Rube
Waddell. He had a great hitting team and a great
defensive squad. The Athletics had won the championship in 1905 and toward the close of the 1907
season it looked as though they were going to take
it again. They had quickly ousted the Tigers from
the rare atmosphere of the league's lead, dropped it
to them for a day late in August, but by the middle of September it looked as if they were just going to walk away with the pennant.

But many a lead which looks safe enough even
as late as mid-September dwindles and evaporates
entirely before the season is out. In recent years
both the St. Louis Cardinals and the then New York

Giants stole the pennant after it had been carefully wrapped up by the old Brooklyn Dodgers. Pittsburgh, to mention only one other team, fell apart in the last weeks of the pennant drive and dropped a comfortable margin and the "sure" pennant.

In 1907 the Tigers took off after the Connie Mackmen and slowly but surely whittled away at what was supposed to be a most comfortable lead —and when the Bengals reached Philadelphia for their final series with the league leaders, the Athletics were leading by a scant three points. This was one series Ty Cobb would never forget. It was the second game—and the last game of what was supposed to be a three-game series—that Ty Cobb pointed to as his greatest day in baseball.

Wild Bill Donovan pitched the first one and the Athletics hit him pretty freely—that is, they cuffed him about pretty well, except when there were A's all over the bases. He gave up thirteen base knocks but the most Philadelphia could do was to score four times. Detroit scored five on its own that afternoon and five was enough to win the game and prized possession of the league's lead.

The Detroit Clubhouse was a madhouse with crazy joy. The Ee-yah man and all his boys cut loose. As far as the Bengals were concerned the race was over and they had the pennant won. But there was one man who did not share in the club's festivities.

He showered and dressed. Then, without so much as a handshake or a simple "so long," he was gone. Sure he was as glad as the next man on the squad that Donovan and the Tigers had won the crucial game. Sure he was as elated as any other Detroiter over the victory with which the team had forged to the front of the American League pennant chase. More than that, he was completely aware of his share in that pennant drive, of his importance to his team in the neck-and-neck race. The fierce pride of accomplishment burned brightly within him, the cockiness of the front-runner gleamed in his eyes. But the animosities burned no less brightly in him, and his hatred for the men who had hazed him so unmercifully in his first years with the Tigers did not diminish. He left the big noise and the big celebration in the clubhouse to walk alone with his sense of victory, his tremendous pride.

That boy, of course, was Tyrus Raymond Cobb, going back to the little hotel—far away from the team—to chat with the little old man who ran the fourth-class inn.

That afternoon, while the rest of the Bengals were whooping it up in brotherly affection, Ty Cobb, the loner, told the story to the little old innkeeper, and that was enough for him. He had no desire for the comradeship of the men with whom he played ball. On the contrary, he avoided it. There was no man who carried his contempt so consistently and for so long.

Of course, that didn't stop him from showing up at the ball park the next afternoon. Nothing short of the grimmest tragedy could keep him away from a ball park. But that afternoon it rained. It rained hard and all day. There was no game, the one-two positions in the American League standings held and the postponed game was shoved up to make a double-header of the last meeting of the two clubs in the 1907 season.

The date was September 30 and Philadelphia's Columbia Park was jammed to the rafters with fans who had come out to see the Mackmen shove the upstart Tigers "back to where they belonged." The Athletics were really burned up about their loss to Donovan and mad enough to tear up the diamond with the Bengals, and their Philadelphia rooters knew it. They came expecting to see the home team slaughter the Tigers, trample them under their feet, end once and for all the threat of the team which only the year before had been buried deep in the second division.

The fans let up a mighty roar as the Athletics took the field. Hartsel was in left field, Seybold in right, Oldring in center, Davis was at first base, Murphy at the keystone sack, Collins at the hot corner, Nicholls at short. Catching was Schreck and in the pitching box the great spitball artist Jim Dygert.

For Detroit it was Jones in left field, Sam (Wahoo) Crawford in center field, the Tyrus in right field, Claude Rossman, one of the best bunters in the game, at first base, Germany Schaefer at second base, Coughlin at third base and O'Leary at shortstop. Behind the bat for the Tigers was Dutch Schmidt and pitching again, after just two days of rest, Wild Bill Donovan.

Connie Mack had Eddie Plank, the immortal Rube Waddell and the mighty Indian Chief Bender to back up his spitball artist. Hughie Jennings had to go down into the barrel before he could get anybody behind Bill Donovan.

Dygert was effective enough in the first inning and the Tigers went down quietly. Not so the Athletics. They took to the wild man as if they owned him, pushing three big runs across the plate before the frame was over. It looked as if the Eeyah man had lost his touch. Certainly Bill Donovan didn't have it. Evidently two days' rest fell short of what the pitcher needed at the tail end of a hectic season.

Detroit managed to get a run back in the second when Jim Dygert messed up the ball a couple of times for a couple of errors. No one could blame him too much. The pressure was on. But when the spitballer walked Donovan to load the bases with Bengals, Connie pulled him out fast and shoved in the great Waddell.

There was only one out and it looked for certain that Detroit was going to catch the off-and-running Athletics. But Rube Waddell was really one of the Hall-of-Famers. He took a couple of warm-up pitches and then promptly struck out Jones and Schaefer, leaving the three men dead on their bases and apparently putting an end to whatever threat the Tigers might have been to the Mackmen's flag aspirations.

When Davis walloped a four-bagger with a man on in the second, the Philadelphia fans roared themselves hoarse. When the Athletics scored two more runs in the fifth, they just settled back in their seats with their popcorn and peanuts to smugly watch the complete annihilation of the Detroit Bengal. The only touch of sentiment they had for any of the Tigers was for Wild Bill Donovan, who originally came from Philadelphia and whose family still lived in the town. They didn't like to see a home town boy slaughtered, even if he was playing for the hated Tigers.

But Hughie Jennings stuck by Bill. They say that he hated to take him out of the box in a Philadelphia game, afraid it might humiliate him in front of his father, his brothers and his old friends. Whatever the reason, the Ee-yah man stuck by Bill Donovan—and it paid off.

In the seventh the Tigers came to life. Oldring muffed an easy one and there was a man on second. Waddell, who had been pitching magnificent ball till then, lost his sight on the plate and walked two of the snarling Bengals to load the bases. Sam Crawford promptly sent home two of them with a grounds-rule double into the overflow crowd of startled Philadelphians. Ty Cobb sent in the third run on a deep smash into the infield and Crawford scored while they were throwing Rossman out at first.

The Tigers were back in the game. The score was seven to five. Philadelphia scored another run in the seventh, Detroit matched it in the eighth. It was still eight to six when the Tigers came up for their last licks in the ninth but then, now or at any other time, the game isn't over till the last man is out and the boys are back in the clubhouse. At least, that's the way the Tigers figured it.

Sam Crawford, the ex-barber from Wahoo, Nebraska, was first man up for the Bengals and he promptly banged out a single.

Ty Cobb followed him to the plate and the Georgia kid had been burning up the league with his bat. As a matter of fact, he was leading the league with his hitting. He was the dangerous hitter. In that ninth inning he was more dangerous, more damaging, than was even suspected.

The Rube looked him over, glanced over to first. He still had a two-run lead and two runs were generally more than enough for the magnificent Waddell. He wound up, let loose with the ball and the Georgia Peach took it.

"Strike one!"

The mighty Waddell wound up, let go again. Ty Cobb knew exactly where it was coming, took one mighty swipe and all Philadelphia gasped as it watched the pellet clear the wooden fences of Columbia Park for a two-run, game-tying four-bagger.

Running out his home run, Tyrus didn't even smile. If there was a hand to greet him, coming into the bench, he didn't see it. Baseball was his job and hitting was part of that job. It was a mighty wallop, that homer, the most important wallop in the whole 1907 season, but Cobb gave no sign, no hint of the great excitement, the exultation churning his insides that afternoon as he rounded the bags.

But later on, many years later on, the Georgia Peach pointed to this memorable September game as his most thrilling day in a long and glorious baseball career. But it was not his home run he credited for the thrill, it was the pitching of Wild Bill Donovan he remembered most.

Donovan, of course, was brilliant that afternoon. He set down the Athletics—the stunned Athletics —in their turn at bat in the ninth and settled down to the kind of pitching which has made him one of the game's immortals.

In the eleventh, Detroit scored once and Philadelphia matched it. From there on in, not a runner could dent that home plate, neither a Tiger nor a Mackman. Seventeen innings the game went and the Athletics, who had ripped Wild Bill for eight runs in seven innings, scored only once in the next ten innings, not once in the last six. It was truly a great exhibition of courage and stamina. With only two days of rest he stood off the mighty Athletics who had to call on three pitchers—Jim Dygert, Rube Waddell and the mighty Plank—for the last eight innings of the game, in order to match the brilliance of baseball's greatest wild man.

Philadelphia never got over the shock of that game, which ended tied because of darkness and left Detroit in first place by a game. The second game scheduled for that afternoon, of course, was wiped off the calendar and the Mackmen never caught up. Jimmy Dygert, who couldn't last against the Bengals, kept the Athletics up there in contention, winning three shut-outs in four days, but the Tigers kept winning and the final standings showed Detroit in first place with a .613 average, Philadelphia in second place with .607. That home run by Ty Cobb in the ninth, tying the game up at eight-eight—and the stamina of Wild Bill Donovan—spelled the difference between the pennant and the runner-up. Ty remembered the great heart of the great pitcher on that historic date. What he knew, although he did not speak of it, was that if he hadn't clouted that ball for all the bases, great heart or no, Donovan would have been beaten and Philadelphia, not Detroit, would have won the pennant in the American League for the year 1907.

The curious fact is that Ty Cobb was a great hitter but home runs were not his specialty, not in 1907. He hit well enough to lead the batting race in the league but there were only five of them that he hit for the distance. And there was no home run he ever hit, before or after, that was more exciting or more telling. It carried the Tigers to the heights of baseball glory and a twenty-year-old hero into his first World Series.

CHAPTER 10

WILD BILL DONOVAN pitched that first game in the 1907 World Series, the first World Series game for the team from Detroit and for the amazing twenty-year-old youngster Ty Cobb.

It was a close game, a squeaker, as Connie Desmond, who broadcasted the Dodger games along with Red Barber, would have said. But most games in those days were of that squeaker variety, one- and two-run affairs, especially in the fall classic between the two pennant winners of the year.

The Bengals had the Cubs three to one when Frankie Chance's boys came up for the last of the ninth inning, and the two runs looked mighty big to the roaring Tigers. They whooped it up in the field and Hughie Jennings was pulling the grass up around the coach's box in personal triumph and letting everybody know about it with his famous Eeyah yell.

But the Chicago Cubs, who had spread-eagled

the whole field in their drive for their pennant, weren't that easily disposed of. Manager Chance, first batter up, belted out a single. Wild Bill Donovan's first pitch hit Steinfeldt in the ribs and there were Cubs on first and second. Joe Tinker, of the most famous of all infield combinations, Tinker to Evers to Chance, popped up, but an error by Coughlin on a routine grounder—which might have ended the game then and there—filled the bases with snarling Bruins and Donovan was in a spot.

He pitched carefully to Schulte, whose infield ball rolled too slowly for a play anywhere but at first base, and Chance scored. There were two away now, a man at second, a man at third. A hit would end the game abruptly and give Chicago a victory where defeat had stared them badly in the face. Bill Donovan set himself to his task and rarely in all of his long and brilliant career in the majors did he ever pitch better. But fate, or luck, or something was set against the wild one and against the Tiger squad that unhappy afternoon in the fall of 1907.

Del Howard was sent up to the plate to pinch-hit for the Cubs, and except for the strange events which followed he might just as well have kept his seat on the bench warm. Twice he went after Wild Bill Donovan's outcurve and twice he fanned the breeze.

Donovan wound up and sent another dancing down the alley and again Del Howard swished his bat and got nothing. The game should have been over right then and there and the Tigers should have been romping back to their clubhouse with their first World Series win in the first World Series game they had ever played. But the ball that Del Howard had missed was missed by someone else who had no business missing it. Dutch Schmidt, the strong man behind the plate, let that Donovan pitch slip right through his big hands and squirt straight for the backstop. He wasn't the strong man then. He was a wild, frantic youngster looking for a passed ball while the Chicago stands went wild and Steinfeldt scampered home to tie up the ball game.

Baseball fans will remember the strike Mickey Owen missed when the Yankees were playing the Dodgers for the 1941 championship, the miss which permitted the New Yorkers to win a lost game and go on to take the series easily. Passed balls are not too uncommon in baseball where the catcher receives a hundred pitches and more during a regulation game. However when a World Series game hinges on it, the passed ball is something that goes down in history, never to be forgotten by the unlucky catcher, the boys who play the game for their bread and butter—and the fans, the eternal fans.

Bill Donovan got Evers trying to steal home that fateful ninth inning and it was Dutch (the unhappy) Schmidt who put the tag on him, but that was all. The game was called at the end of the twelfth inning because of darkness. It was the closest the Detroit Tigers came to victory in that 1907 classic. It was their best day in the series. The Cubs took the Bengals, after that first game, the way they had taken the National League flag. It was no contest at all. The Cubs won every game and the Bengals went back to their winter sports and winter jobs a very disappointed lot. And no one was more disappointed than the kid from Georgia.

They had presented him with a diamond-studded gold medal for his brilliant hitting in the regulation season, but all he could do in the World Series was to collect himself a lowly batting average of .200. Nor had he stolen a single base. Hughie Jennings had predicted early in the season that Tyrus Raymond Cobb would prove the greatest baseball player in the game, while Frankie Chance, whatever insults he hurled during the games, had feared Ty Cobb more than any other single man on the Detroit squad. But in the series he had been anything but great and Chance had had precious little to worry about. Ty Cobb was a thoroughly unhappy boy as he took the train back to Georgia. He would have liked to start the series all over again. If he could only take another swing at something some Cub hurler would slant down at him at the plate. But that would have to wait now. That would have to wait till next year. It never occurred to the young Cobb that there might not be a next year, that the Tigers might not repeat. He was too cocky a youngster to think anything else.

Of course, there was no real reason for Ty Cobb to fret. In the 1907 season he had come of age, baseballwise. He hadn't reached the voting age of twenty-one yet, but he had led his league in batting, clouting the ball at a tremendous .350

clip. He had led the league with two hundred and twelve solid safeties—twenty-nine of which were two-baggers—fifteen triples and five for the distance. He had let everyone know that he was the kingpin in the batter's box and that he intended to stay kingpin. And he also stole the greatest number of bases in the league for the 1907 seasons, pilfering forty-nine of them.

It had been a sensational year for Cobb, the kid who had to battle not only the opposition in the American circuit, but all of his own teammates as well, in his determined fight to stay in the leagues and in baseball. It had been a great year for the young loner. But it was only the beginning of one of the most exciting careers in baseball's long and exciting story.

TY COBB never had any doubt about his ability to play the game. Nor did he ever doubt his importance to his team. He had been a cocky youngster when he played the infield for the Royston Rompers. Now at twenty-one he was more brash, more belligerent than ever as he sent back the contract Frank Navin offered him to play ball for the 1908 Detroit Tigers.

"I led the league in hitting," he wrote to the Detroit office. "I stole more bases than anyone else in the league. The contract you sent me doesn't begin to offer me what I'm worth to the club. I won't consider anything less than five thousand dollars for the year."

There was no question of the Georgian's value to the team in dollars and cents. There wouldn't have been the Detroit pennant without Ty Cobb in the field. But five thousand dollars in 1908 was a big heap of money and the baseball front office wasn't paying out that kind of money, not if it could help it. The Detroit Bengals started their training sessions in Arkansas that spring without their pugnacious Georgian.

But they also started it without George Mullin and without their first sacker Rossman. Ty Cobb's demands for the big boost in his salary got a good press and his insistence on a proportionate share of the good fortunes of his club stimulated the rest of the boys on the club to set up a big holler for a big wage hike. Nor did the general cry for bigger contracts stop with the Detroit Club. The Cobb fever spread like wildfire through both leagues, and even players like Hans Wagner, the all-time great shortstop of the Pittsburgh Pirates, who had never given Barney Dreyfuss, owner of the Corsairs, any contract trouble, held out for a good deal more than the five thousand dollars he was getting after burning up the infield in the Smoky City for twelve full years.

The owners in both circuits reacted sharply. Statements in the press were a dime a dozen. This upstart Georgian had touched off a dynamite keg. There had been individual hold-outs before, and some stubborn ones, but there had never been such a mass uprising on the part of the boys who played the game for the scaling up of their contract prices.

"All I want," said Cobb, "is what I deserve. I don't want anything more and I don't think I'm being unreasonable."

"The creation cannot be greater than the creator," came back Frank Navin. "Cobb is not bigger than baseball."

The fans took a hand. The fans always take a hand. The furor was much like the rumpus that hit the press and the people when Babe Ruth, much later, had his titanic salary struggles with Colonel Ruppert of the New York Yankees. The salaries the Bambino fought for were considerably higher than the five thousand dollars the Georgian demanded but the bitterness, the rancor and the heat engendered were no less.

"I'm ready to quit baseball," said Cobb, and he was.

"I want security," he said. "I don't know for how long I'll be any good on the diamond. I might get hurt—anybody can get hurt playing the game—and then I'll be through. As long as I'm there, I want to get everything due me."

That was the spirit and the argument of the ballplayers on every club in both leagues. The game was tough. It was dangerous, too. A duster might get too close and bang a man in the skull, finishing him for everything and everyone. A hard slide and a broken ankle, a tough chance and a broken arm or a broken leg—and the ballplayer making himself five thousand dollars for the year wasn't worth a nickel to his club.

The Tigers had almost finished their training in Little Rock that year before they finally came to terms with the boy they knew they had to have if they were going to try to cop the American League pennant again in 1908.

They didn't give him the five thousand dollars he had held out for, but they did boost his salary a full two thousand and Ty Cobb signed for forty-five hundred. This was quite a hike for the Georgian, who had played for two hundred and fifty a month in 1906 and four hundred a month in 1907. More important, as far as baseball history is concerned, it was the beginning of the big check for the professional ballplayer. There can be no doubt that the four- and five-figure salaries players have drawn and continue to draw in the big time had their beginnings in the fight Ty Cobb led for decent contracts way back in 1908. As a matter of fact, it was the Georgian himself who eventually pulled one of the fancier salaries in the story of the game. In 1920 the Georgia Peach was holding down a forty-thousand-dollar job in baseball. It was the fattest pay check in the game and there was no one who ever deserved it more.

The Tigers, of course, soon forgot their conflict with the belligerent Georgian and settled down to the business of fighting for the 1908 flag. And that season, much like the 1907 race, was a humdinger and the Detroit Club was not sorry in the least that Cobb hadn't quit the game for college or some business career. They needed him badly and without him they wouldn't have been anywhere near the top in the dramatic struggle for the league championship. He gave them their forty-five hundred dollars' worth—and more.

There were four teams in the race that year,

Chicago's White Sox, Cleveland's Naps, the Browns from St. Louis, aided considerably by the acquisiton of Rube Waddell from the Athletics, and the 1907 pennant winners, the Detroit Tigers. For a short spell Clark Griffith's New Yorkers held the lead but soon went into a tail spin and finished in the cellar. Nor could St. Louis, for all of Waddell's heroic efforts, keep the pace. The other three teams, however, battled it down to the wire.

The great Ed Walsh won forty games that year for the Chicago White Sox. He pitched four hundred and sixty-four innings and played in sixty-six games, a phenomenal feat. If it weren't for Addie Joss and the no-hit, no-run game he pitched for the Naps against the magnificent Walsh, the powder puff hitters from the Windy City would have copped again in 1908. Ed had limited the Clevelanders to but one run, but it was one run too many in that crucial game and it cost Chicago the flag.

Cleveland, too, fizzled when they had the pennant in their hands—and the league's lead in the final standing came down to the last game in the season.

Wild Bill Donovan of the Tigers faced the White Sox knowing that the winner of the game would go into the World Series, while the loser would drop to third, behind the unfortunate, idle Naps. And he pitched one of his more brilliant games that afternoon while the Georgia Peach hammered out a triple and two singles. It was a runaway performance. Chicago was blanked while the Tigers came in with seven solid runs to win the American League pennant.

It was a great win and a great season for the Detroit Tigers. It was another great season for the Georgia Peach. For the second year in succession he led the league in batting with a lusty .324. It wasn't his greatest batting year. As a matter of fact, it was the lowest batting mark he made for the records in twenty years of baseball. Only in his final season of 1928, at the age of forty-two, did he fall lower to a mere .323. But in 1908 his .324 was big enough to make him tops in the hitting department. It might be well to remember at this time that the rabbit ball was still a long way off, that balls didn't clear the fences as regularly as they do today. Even clouters like Sam Crawford hit the home run infrequently and Sam could clout well enough to reach the walls with one of the deadest balls in the game—and did it with clocklike regularity.

But Ty wasn't the reputed long ball hitter, even in those days. He had hit five homers in 1907. He hit only four of them in 1908. However, he led his league in every other hitting department. He had the most hits, one hundred and eighty-eight. He had the most doubles, thirty-six. And he had banged out the most triples, twenty. He also stole thirty-nine bases that year.

Certainly it had been a stupendous year for Cobb and the Tigers knew that they hadn't paid the Georgian too much for his year's work. He was worth every bit of that forty-five hundred dollars his contract called for—and a whole lot more.

To make that emphatic, the Georgia Peach put on a little extra display of his value to the Bengals in the series for the World's Championship.

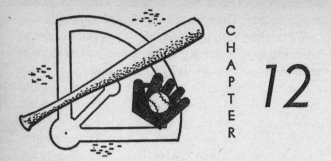

THE Chicago Cubs had again won the pennant in the National League, but this time they hadn't run away from the rest of the circuit. As a matter of record, if it hadn't been for the most remembered of all boners in baseball, the Detroit Tigers should have faced the Little Napoleon John McGraw's Giants in the fall classic. But Fred Merkle of the Giants had forgotten to touch second base and the pennant-winning game which the New York team thought it had won was ruled a one-one tie. In 1908 there were still a lot of rules that needed to be written into the Official Rule Book. Germany Schaefer, for example, that stanch comedian of the Detroit Tigers—who used to pull a goatee out of his pocket to get a big laugh out of the crowds, and who was the first man in a baseball uniform to come to bat in a raincoat and carry an umbrella in protest against the weather and the umpires—once stole first base. It seems that he couldn't get a rise out of the pitcher from where he was perched on second, so he stole first from where he could heckle better. That made one for the Rule Book—and after the comic Schaefer's feat, stealing first from second, or any other base in reverse, was outlawed.

The touching of second base by a runner from first on a hit which scores a winning run in the last licks of the home team was passed over lightly in the old days. It was generally considered enough for the run to come in and the batter to reach first. But the cantankerous Johnny Evers of the Chicago Cubs had that all changed when he argued vociferously and effectively that Fred Merkle was forced at second for the third out of the inning, and that therefore the run the Giants thought they had scored had not been scored at all.

The Giants yelled their heads off but it was no go and the Giants and the Cubs were forced into a play-off game for the National League bunting. The Cubs took it. The Giants got special medals issued by the New York office to the effect that they were the real champions, but it was the Chicago team which got into the World Series.

With the tightness of the National League race and the improvement in the Tiger squad, there were great hopes in the automobile town and in every other American League city that this time the Bengals would avenge their disgraceful defeat in the 1907 classic. Among the new players in the Detroit squad was Owen J. (Donie) Bush, the kid shortstop from Indianapolis, one of the scrappiest infielders of all time, a five-foot-six pint-sizer. He more than made up for what he lacked in height with his brilliant covering of the key spot in the infield, as well as with his ability to get that base on balls and hit in the clutches. Of course, the big threat with the tigers was their twenty-one-year-old Tyrus Raymond Cobb.

Cobb had had a miserable time in the 1907 classic but he gave notice immediately that 1908 was another year and that history for once wasn't going to be repeated.

In the very first inning of the first game of the series against the Cubs, McIntyre promptly set the Detroit fans roaring with a clean single. They roared again as he stole second. The stands went wild when Ty Cobb sent him home promptly with a clean hit through the middle.

But there wasn't much more cheering for Detroit's fans that day as the Bengals slipped all over a rain-drenched field and the Cubs romped in to win the first game over the fumbling Tigers by the score of ten to six.

Nor could the Bengals stop the Cubs from taking the second game of the 1908 classic. Wild Bill Donovan faced only twenty-two Cubs in the first seven innings of that game, but the storm came up in the eighth and the Cubs scored six times before they were finally set down. It was Ty Cobb's single in the ninth, scoring pinch-hitter Jones, which counted the only run the Tigers collected in that unfortunate set-to.

In the third game of the series the Tigers finally came to life, and the spearhead was the pugnacious

Georgian who punched out a double and three singles for a brilliant World Series performance, giving Detroit its first series victory.

But that was all for the Tigers. The Cubs picked up the next two and for the second year in succession the Chicago team had beaten the Detroit Tigers for the World Championship. In their third win of the classic, which was played in one hour and thirty-five minutes, three-fingered Mordecai Brown set down the Tigers with just four hits and no runs at all. The fifth and final game proved an even more humiliating defeat for the Bengals. Cub ace pitcher Overall got two runs from his Chicago teammates and that was one more than he needed. Detroit came nowhere near the home plate after one of the most bizarre first, last or any inning in World Series history.

Overall, who sometimes had difficulty finding the plate but was as tough a pitcher as you can find in the clutches, had himself quite a time in that first inning. He walked McIntyre to start things off, then fanned O'Leary. Wahoo Crawford singled, sending McIntyre to second. With two men on base and dangerous Ty Cobb at bat, it looked like early curtains for the Cub hurler. He worked the corners carefully, and he got the anxious Cobb swinging at a third strike. There were still two on and with Claude Rossman, one of the wiliest of hitters at bat, the Detroit fans were still yelling for pitcher Overall's head. Nor did the crafty Rossman disappoint the crowd. Claude was always doing the unexpected. This was the spot in which he did it again.

Overall was overpowering. He got two quick strikes on the Tiger first baseman. His third pitch was wild but Rossman quick on the trigger, swung at the ball which the catcher couldn't possibly hold and was off to first, making it easily.

Three men had been struck out by the erratic Cub pitcher. There was just one hit, but the bases were loaded with Tigers and that Prince of Clowns Germany Schaefer marched up to the plate swinging his war club, intent on committing mayhem. And all Detroit was behind him.

But Overall was master again and Germany couldn't see the ball at all. He swung at a fast one—missed. Missed another for strike two.

"Strike three! You're out!"

Overall had to strike out four men that inning to retire the side, but he did it, and from then on in only one other Tiger was able to clip him for a hit. The final score of another miserable series for the Tigers: Chicago two, Detroit nothing.

Seven hits and no runs in two games was the record for the Bengals in the 1908 classic. Everyone was down in the mouth, everyone but Hughie Jennings and Ty Cobb.

"A great team beat us!" the fiery manager declared to the boys draped and drooped around the clubhouse, and he meant it.

For Ty Cobb there was his season's record to remember, a brilliant record. There was also the satisfaction of knowing the series—whatever it had been for Detroit—was a personal triumph for himself. Where he had batted a lowly .200 in the 1907 series, in the 1908 classic he had smashed out seven solid blows for a magnificent average of .368. He had almost doubled his average of the year before, scored three runs where the year before he had scored only once—and had stolen a couple bases where the year before he couldn't steal a single sack.

He was twenty-one in 1908 and his baseball career, barely begun, was already brilliant. Ty Cobb had much to be pleased with, despite the fiasco of the World Series. But there was something else besides baseball on his mind that year. Ty Cobb—the cocky, haughty, pugnacious kid wonder of the diamond, freely hated and freely admired, easily aroused and quick with his fists, the Georgia Peach —was in love.

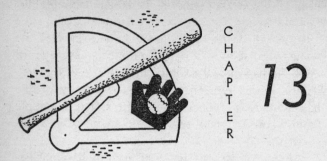

HER name was Charlotte Lombard and she was a
baseball fan. She was one of the Augusta girls who
flocked to see the local South Atlantic League team
on its regularly scheduled Ladies' Days. It was there
that the dark-haired beauty first saw young Tyrus
Raymond Cobb and fell in love with him.

It was quite the thing for the young society
belles of Augusta to crowd around the star ballplayers after the game, talk about the game and
ask the young men to join them in some evening
get-together.

"Wouldn't you like to join us?" asked the young,
lovely and very wealthy Miss Lombard.

Ty looked at the girl quizzically. She was big
city stuff for the boy who came from Royston. He
wasn't quite used to big city ways and manners. He
looked at his pal Nap Rucker. Nap came from another small hamlet in Georgia. Crabapple was home
to Rucker and Crabapple girls didn't dress as fan-
cily as the girls in Augusta. Nor did they talk as

easily to the boys. Nap was no help to the Peach, none at all.

"Come on, boys," chorused the Augusta bevy of beauties. "It's fun! Lots of fun!"

But Tyrus shook his head and Nap Rucker shook his, too.

"Not this time, thanks."

"Sure?" asked the pretty Charlotte Lombard.

"Some other day," said Ty.

And then when he was alone with Nap he could have kicked himself.

"Why didn't you want to go?" he demanded.

"I didn't say anything," protested Nap.

"No, you didn't!" came back Tyrus. "But you looked scared enough!"

But Ty and Charlotte met one early evening, at the swimming pool at the edge of town, and the wall between the city girl and the country boy began to crumble.

"Does your father know you go out to the ball game—and does he mind your going out with a ballplayer?"

Charlotte turned to look at the young Tyrus quizzically.

"And why shouldn't he know?" she asked.

Ty picked up a pebble, tossed it into the water and watched the ripples.

"I don't know," he said, finally.

And Charlotte laughed and Ty laughed and the romance moved forward quickly.

"Where are you going from Augusta?" asked Miss Lombard.

"The big leagues, I suppose," said Tyrus.

"You'll be there soon," said the young enthusiast.

"I hope so," smiled Ty.

"I know you will," insisted the Augusta belle. "You're the best ballplayer Augusta has ever had. You're in a class all by yourself, Tyrus."

He smiled.

"It's nice to hear you say that."

"It's true. It's just the truth."

Her eyes sparkled. Her mouth was a bright red.

"You're sweet," said the young Cobb.

Charlotte blushed, turned her face. She couldn't say what was on her mind. She couldn't say what was on her tongue. An Augusta girl might be enthusiastic about baseball. She might even go out with ballplayers to sit around the edge of a pool at the edge of town. But there were some things a young lady could not say.

"We'll be in Augusta till Monday," said Ty. "Can we go riding again?"

Charlotte searched the eyes of the young ball hawk.

"Of course," she said.

They hired a hack and drove out to the swimming place.

"Tomorrow?" said Ty.

Charlotte smiled.

"Tomorrow."

And there were many tomorrows. Soon the Peach was calling at her home—and when Ty went up to Detroit there was a warm and tender spot in his heart for a beautiful dark-haired girl in Augusta.

In 1908 they were married. Charlotte Lombard became Charlotte Cobb and for many, many long years she gave the Peach the things he yearned for most in life—love and a home. They had five children—Tyrus, Jr., Herschel, Beverly, Howell and Shirley—and while Tyrus Cobb may have been a demon in a ball park, a terror to all men, with children he was as soft as butter and sweeter than brown sugar.

"I love my home and my wife and children," the Peach once told that great American novelist Theodore Dreiser. "And somehow a home without a yard or a little of the country around it never seemed quite right to me. . . . I'm a great family man really, and I want my kids to have the proper home surroundings. My home means everything to me. And when I'm through at night I want to go there."

There was a lot the Peach had missed as a kid. The stern Herschel had never shown him any affection. He was a disciplinarian, always scolding—and because of that Ty made up for it with his own family.

"I get an awful lot of fun and happiness just playing with my children," he said. "It's a relief for me to come home and take an interest in what they're doing."

They climbed all over him—and there was a lot to climb over.

"Have you been a good girl, Beverly?"

"Did you help mother shop, son?"

"That's a mighty pretty dress, Shirley."

"I want my children to be close to me," he said. "I was starved for affection when I was a kid, and I know how much it means."

And Charlotte Cobb gazed fondly at her husband sitting at the head of the table, doting on the children.

He's the biggest baby I've got, she thought.

He was the toughest man on the diamond. He was the softest, warmest, kindest man at home.

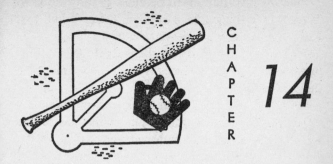

C
H
A
P
T
E
R

14

THE year 1909 was another exciting, dramatic, hectic year for both the Detroit Tigers and their great star Ty Cobb. This time it was a rejuvenated Philadelphia club which was to battle them down to the wire for the American League pennant, a team jam-packed with brilliant youngsters. Eddie Collins was with them. Frank Baker, who was going to be nicknamed Home-run Baker, was playing third base for Connie Mack. There was Jack Barry and Jack Coombs, both of whom would leave their mark on the game. In the Philadelphia pitching department—in addition to Coombs—there were the old stand-bys, such great names as Chief Bender and Eddie Plank. Rube Oldring and Danny Murphy were in the outfield. Harry Davis was at first. It was quite a team to start with, but when Connie brought in Lefty Krause, the Californian Collegian, to give up a scant five runs in the first ten games he pitched in the majors, and win them all, the Philadelphia Macks were all but unbeatable.

To do the trick, Hughie Jennings did a bit of revamping on his own. Coughlin, O'Leary and Germany Schaefer were dropped and a sparkling new infield did its stuff for the Bengals in 1909. Foremost among the new faces was the new third baseman George Moriarty, as pugnacious and aggressive a player as ever wore a Bengal uniform. Not only was he brilliant in the field but he was equally brilliant on the base paths, stealing home half a dozen times in his first season with Detroit. Donie Bush, who had appeared late in the 1908 season, was good enough for shortstop, but Tom Jomes replaced Rossman at first and Jimmy Delahanty, whose vocabulary might shock the more sensitive ears, took over second from Germany Schaefer. And they all did very well.

Philadelphia, however, was doing all right, too. As a matter of fact, when the Mackmen came into Detroit for a three-game series as late as August 24, Connie's men and not the Tigers were leading the league.

It was in the first of these games that the ever-dramatic Ty Cobb became a national issue again. In 1908 it was his demand for a substantial increase in salary which had set off the fireworks. This time it was the spirit, the fire, the win-or-die determination of the fierce Georgian which hit the headlines.

Everyone in baseball, players and spectators alike, knew how dangerous a man Ty Cobb was with the bat. They also knew how dangerous a man he was on the bases. On the base paths he was perhaps the worst hazard an opposing pitcher had to contend with. There was no telling when he was suddenly going to dart for second or third or even home. He was never still on the base, once he got there. He always wanted that extra one, and more often than anyone else in the game he took it. Sometimes he would announce it in advance.

"I'm stealing second on your next pitch, you old goat!"

And he did.

Many a top-notch catcher, when asked how to keep Ty Cobb from stealing a bag, would advise the rookie catcher to throw to the bag ahead of the one which was the Georgian's immediate goal.

"If you know he's heading for second," they said, seriously enough, "peg it down to third."

The young catcher might raise his eyebrows skeptically, but the old catcher would still be deadly earnest, concluding, "You've only got one chance. He might be going on to third and then you've got him nabbed."

Sound as that strategy might have seemed, it nevertheless didn't always work. The Georgia Peach, once on first, was a demon who was almost impossible to handle. On a sacrifice bunt it was quite normal for the Flash to slide into third— safe. It was common practice for a rival first baseman to peg to third base hoping to get Ty coming into the bag. It should have worked because Cobb wasn't the man to tarry at second very long, and with almost any other man who

101

ever played ball it would have worked. Not with Ty Cobb.

With the sacrifice bunt, Ty was off and running. The play, of course, went to first, and then, quickly across the diamond, the ball was snapped to third. Easily and confidently the third sacker reached down to tag out the oncoming Bengal. But instead of the Bengal there was nothing but air —and before the surprised player at the hot corner could recover his equilibrium, there was Ty Cobb coming into home plate standing up!

We don't see that happen much these days, a man coming home to score from first on a sacrifice bunt. But there was only one Ty Cobb.

He was the most unnerving man on base, as far as the opposing pitchers were concerned. He wasn't too easy on the opposing infielders either.

Cobb pulled out all the psychological stops. He knew best how to get at a pitcher. His trick for getting at the infielders was perhaps a bit brutal but it worked, and the Peach felt that anything that worked to his advantage—and to the advantage of his team on the field—was something to be practiced constantly and consistently.

He ran the bases fast. He also ran them furiously. This was common knowledge in the baseball world. He practiced long hours in the sliding pit, perfecting every possible slide to a bag. Off the field he walked around in heavily leaded shoes, just so that he could be lighter on his feet during a game. It was much like the manner in which he carried two and three bats to the plate before he chose one with which to do his clouting. At that time players and fans thought it was just an attention-seeking stunt on the part of the Georgian, but the stunt paid off in base hits. He was, incidentally, the first man in baseball to approach the plate with weighted hands. It made swinging that much lighter, that much easier. Today, everybody in baseball goes up to bat with a couple of bats in his hands, and for the same reason. Ty Cobb studied every angle of the game, studied it like a scientist, to improve every department of the game, especially those departments which concerned him most.

From the psychological angle it was his base stealing which drove a considerable number of rookies almost frantic with fear of the flying Georgian. He had his effect, too, on even the most seasoned of ballplayers.

Ty's neat little trick was to take a prominent seat in front of the dugout before game time—prominent, that is, to all the boys who would be playing against him. Then, comfortably seated, he would take out his spiked shoes and begin to hone them. And he honed down those spikes till they were nearly as sharp as a well-honed razor. The men playing against him would turn away, or try to turn away, but Ty Cobb got the effect he wanted. Everybody knew that when the Georgian came sliding for a base, and he came sliding into the bases regularly and persistently, he was always there with his spikes flashing in the sun. And they would be brilliant in the afternoon sun, the way he had honed them before game time. Many of the young players, and even the older and more fearless of them, chilled just a bit watching Cobb perform on his spikes in front of the Bengal dugout. And there was reason enough for the chill.

Frank Baker knew it that afternoon of August 24, 1909, when the league-leading Philadelphia Athletics came in for a three-game series with the second-place Tigers.

As the fierce Georgian came sliding into the guarded third base, Frankie got the ball and put it on him, but the play was costly. There was a deep, nasty gash in his right arm, just under the elbow, where he had made contact with those razor-sharp spikes of the Peach.

There were no blows on the field and Frank Baker continued to play after he had been well bandaged by the Philadelphia trainer. But the blows off the field, in the press, around the leagues and wherever fans collected were fast, furious and plenty loud.

There was some support—or rather defense—of the Georgian fury, but the anti-Cobb forces all but drowned it out.

"He doesn't hone those spikes for exercise!"

"Take Cobb out before he cripples the whole American League!"

"It's time someone put a stop to the way Ty Cobb intimidates every infielder in the game!"

"Stop him before he murders someone!"

"It's all part of the game," answered the unfrightened Cobb. "A man plays the game as hard as he can play it or he doesn't play it at all. You've got to give everything you've got or else you don't deserve the salary you're getting."

"Play it hard," came back the anti-Cobb forces. "But what have honed spikes got to do with playing the game?"

"I'll do everything and anything that's legal to get as many bases as I can in the game. That's what I'm in the game for," snapped back the Georgia Peach.

"But spiking a man isn't legal," charged the Cobb critics.

"I was out to take third," shot back Tyrus, "not to spike Baker. He was spiked but that wasn't my fault. The base runner has first right to the base paths. That's where his bread and butter is. Part of it anyway. It's up to the man guarding the base to protect it the best way he can, but no one can take away the base runner's right to the base paths."

There wasn't much anyone could say in reply to that argument on the part of the Georgian who had been pressed by his father to follow the legal profession. The Peach knew how to argue a point, knew how to do it well enough to stump any of his coherent would-be opponents. But logic doesn't always rule among the fans and the spiking of Frank Baker was not soon forgotten by the good and rabid people of Philadelphia.

Detroit swept that three-game series, swept the Mackmen out of the league's lead and, as a result, became the top running team in the American

League. It was a lead the Bengals held and increased until they were a good three and a half games in front of the Athletics when the Tigers walked into Shibe Park for their final meetings of the season.

Feelings ran pretty high in Philadelphia, and for more than one reason. First, if Connie Mack's boys duplicated the Detroit trick of August 24th, 25th and 26th, in reverse, and swept the series from the Bengals, it would be the Mackmen again in first place. That was cause enough for the high tension which jammed the ball park for the crucial games. But there was an added attraction. Ty Cobb was going to be in the ball park and all the pent-up hatred for the Tigers in general, and the Georgian in particular, flared up.

First there were the bushels of letters and post cards and telegrams in which the Peach was called everything from a no-good to an out-and-out murderer, as well as a few names that can't be printed in a family newspaper. Then there was the particular telegram, the omnious telegram, which threatened Ty Cobb with sudden death if he so much as showed his face in Shibe Park. Death would come from a bullet fired from outside the playing grounds.

This same threat of violence came to the Georgian not once but many times, worded differently but with the same intention, the same warning and the same threat.

Ty Cobb wasn't particuarly worried. He showed

The youthful Cobb in 1915   UPI

Getting set to go after a long ball

The classic swing

Belting a long one

Another stolen base

Ty Cobb, Connie Mack, and Howard Ehmke

At 1925 World Series—Ty Cobb, Babe Adams, and Hans Wagner

UPI

At home on his 62nd birthday, 1950

Jennings some of the messages and laughed them off.

"Crackpots," said Ty Cobb, scornfully.

"You're going to play?" asked the manager.

The Georgian looked at him curiously.

"What do you think my blood's made of?" he asked.

His eyes sharpened, his chin jutted out. He was mad.

"Try to keep me off that field!" he shouted. "I'll show them the kind of stuff Ty Cobb's made of!"

But Hughie Jennings was genuinely worried. He showed Connie Mack some of the fan mail Cobb was getting and Connie acted with dispatch. He had no love for Ty Cobb but he didn't want to see murder committed in his ball park.

No one in baseball was ever as well protected as was the Georgia Peach during that series in Philadelphia. He was escorted by police to the park and escorted home after the game. There was a squadron of police between Ty Cobb in the field and the fans behind him. There were policemen, plain-clothes men scattered through the park and a squad of riflemen on the roofs surrounding the arena. Nothing was going to happen to Ty Cobb by way of a bullet, even a stray bullet, if Connie Mack and the Philadelphia Police Force could help it.

And nothing did happen to the Georgia Peach during that series.

As to the series, the Mackmen took the first one from the tightened Tigers two to one, Eddie Plank pitching one of his normally brilliant games, while the fans jeered and hooted at Ty Cobb for all they were worth.

The Tigers took the second, five to three, with George Mullin pitching brilliantly, and the only fun the Philadelphians in the stand had was their unrelenting badgering of Ty Cobb. It was the game that counted, the only game the Tigers took in the series but enough to enable them to leave the City of Brotherly Love with a lead of a game and a half, despite two consecutive victories by Connie Mack's Chief Bender and, again, Eddie Plank.

And that game and a half was enough, as things developed, for the Tigers to win their third American League pennant in as many years. As for Cobb, he continued to believe that the base paths belonged to him and he continued to run them that way. He got his own lumps, and plenty. His body and his legs, especially, were just a solid mass of rips and tears and bruises, but he never complained. It was part of the game and that's the way he played it.

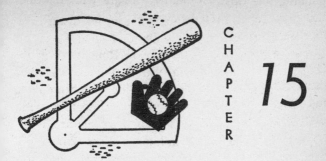

FOR the third time in as many years, Ty Cobb was the top batter in the American League's regular season of 1909. He was beginning to make it a habit and that habit was going to stick for a long time. At bat five hundred and seventy-three times officially, the Georgia Peach hammered out a colossal two hundred and sixteen hits, and that was better than anyone else wearing an American League uniform could do until the Georgian himself bettered it with two hundred and forty-eight good clouts two years later, in 1911. Where in 1908 he had won the batting crown with .324, the Cobb came back with a tremendous average of .377 to take the crown again. He also scored the greatest number of runs for the Detroit Tigers, a neat one hundred and sixteen, and for the first and only time in his brilliant career he led the league in home runs. The total wasn't great. Judged by the way the ball is smacked out of the parks with almost monotonous regularity these days, the home

109

run mark made by the Peach was meager. The exact number of balls he hit for the distance in 1909 was the lowly, lowly figure of nine. This is no misprint. Nine, spelled out or in Roman numerals, comes to the same thing. But hitting nine homers in a season before the era of the Bambino Ruth and the rabbit ball was quite a respectable feat. It was enough to name Ty Cobb the leading home run hitter in the American League in the year 1909.

No one could ever say that the Georgia Peach couldn't clout them for the distance if he wanted to. He walloped out enough doubles and triples in his lifetime of ball playing to dispel any rumor to that effect. The point was, and still is, that the era in which Ty Cobb played—the hit, the sacrifice, the daring run on the base paths, the Texas-leaguer, the ball placed in the right spot at the right time so that no fielder could get his glove on it—these, and not the long ball out of the park, made up the strategy and tactics which meant the difference between a game won or lost.

The Peach never did have much respect for either the power hitters or for the rabbit ball which brought an epidemic of them into the game. He wasn't one of those who worshiped the mighty Babe Ruth. On the contrary, he didn't like George Herman at all, and on two counts. First, it was Cobb's general antipathy for the four-base smack which blew a close game wide open. Second, he didn't enjoy watching his fans' great attraction for him slowly fade away as bigger and bigger stadiums were being constructed to oblige the tens of thousands of baseball enthusiasts who clamored to watch the great Babe smite the apple out of the ball park.

Cobb didn't mind watching the ferocious Jack Dempsey slug a man unconscious with his brutal fists. He rather enjoyed it. He certainly appreciated the slugging of his fellow Georgian Bobby Jones on the golf links. As far as the Peach was concerned, the era of slugging was all right anywhere except on the baseball diamond. There he wanted the psychological duel between the pitcher and the batter. There he wanted the surprise bunt and the swift dash for the unprotected bag. There he wanted the suspense, the one-run margin, the man on the middle sack poised to come dashing home, the threat of a steal, the quick throw to second, the snap relay to first. He wanted all the facets of the game which made it a play of intuition, mind strategy.

Much of that still remains on the diamond, of course, but there can be no doubt that the home run can and often does overwhelm the smartest managing, the smartest coaching, the sharpest hitting and the most brilliant base running. The Georgia Peach didn't like the home run the way the Babe was hitting it. He liked even less the adulation heaped on the boy who had come from Baltimore's St. Mary's Orphanage to make baseball history.

"Anyone can hit the ball over the fence," he said, when asked about the big Ruth's prodigious

111

clouting. "Can he lay down a bunt? Can he put it where nobody ain't?"

"He doesn't have to lay down a bunt," came the rejoinder "and where he puts them they never come back."

The Peach glared.

"Everybody's hitting them where they never come back. That home run's so cheap, it's cheaper than a dozen of last week's rolls at the bakery."

This was early in 1925. Cobb had been in the big leagues for a long time then. It was his *twentieth* season with the Detroit Tigers. There weren't too many years in baseball left to him, but there were enough to let him tell the fans everywhere and in a language they could understand, that Babe Ruth wasn't the only man who could put them out of the park, that there was a man by the name of Ty Cobb who could send them into the bleachers as easily, if only he wanted to.

Detroit was playing St. Louis and the Peach let loose. Three times that afternoon he poled the ball for all the bases, three times he hit the apple out for all the sacks—three homers in one game, something that hadn't been done in big-league baseball since the turn of the century. Bobby Lowe had done it for the Boston Braves in 1894. Ed Delehanty had done it for Philadelphia in 1896. Ty Cobb was next, in 1925. And this was after the great Bambino had established himself as the greatest four-base clouter of all time.

The stands cheered the Georgian to the rafters. The Detroit squad slapped his back and shook his hand till it hurt. Even the St. Louis Browns stopped to applaud the old man, for as far as baseball is concerned Ty was a very aged outfielder. The Georgia Peach? He just shrugged it off.

"Anybody can do it. Everybody's doing it. What's the big noise? Nothing but a long fungo. Here! Go out and do it yourself."

And the next day, to show that it wasn't a fluke, he hit two more for the distance.

"If they want homers, I'll give them homers till they're sick of them."

But Tyrus was just mad. He loved the game too much to be facetious about it. And he liked the game the hard way. He hit five out of the park in two days, a colossal feat in those or any other days of the game. But he went back to strategic hitting, for that was where his heart was, and there were just seven more of them which he hit out of the park for that entire season.

In 1909 he led the league with nine homers. In that year he also led the league in stolen bases with the phenomenal mark of seventy-six. His honed spikes helped, no doubt, but it was his great speed on the base paths and his great love for the drama of the game which were the basic ingredients of his base-stealing records. In 1911 he stole eighty-three of them. In 1915 he stole an almost unbelievable ninety-six. All in all, Ty Cobb stole eight hundred and ninety-two bases in his major league career, twenty-seven of them when he was past forty years old. What a magnificent record! What a record for ballplayers to shoot at! What an inspiring record for everybody who plays the game—from the kid making that fall-away slide on some sandlot anywhere in these United States, to all the Maury Willses and Lou Brocks shooting up the dust around second base in every major league park in the country!

IN THEIR first two World Series, Hughie Jennings
and his Detroit Tigers, despite the pressure of
their Georgia star Ty Cobb, had taken a pretty
awful beating. In the first classic, that of 1907, all
they had been able to do was to tie one game. In
1908 they managed to take one victory, but nothing
more. Of course, the Chicago Cubs, who administered the beating in each series, were a pretty classy
outfit, one of the best clubs ever assembled in the
National League, or in the American League too,
for that matter. The Cubs won one hundred and
four games in the 1909 season and that many
games in the victory column is generally more than
enough to insure a pennant. It wasn't in 1909, not
by six and a half games, for it was the Pittsburgh
Pirates, the Barney Dreyfuss Club, which led the
senior circuit that year with a phenomenal record
of one hundred and ten victories.

The Cubs of 1907 had won one hundred and
sixteen games. There hadn't been a team in the

National League to challenge them. And they had slashed the Bengals to ribbons in the fall classic. The Pittsburgh Pirates promised to do no less in their World Series of 1909 with the three-time winner of the American League flag. And the Detroit fans, for all their wishful thinking, hoping and confidence, were a little weak in the knees at the approaching battle for the World Championship.

The first game of the classic was played in Pittsburgh and, right out of the hat, the Pirate's crafty manager Fred Clarke pulled a fast one which was to pay off with that extra dividend. Instead of starting his ace hurler Howard Camnitz, known throughout the baseball world at the time as the Kentucky Rosebud, the Corsair manager stuck his first-year pitcher, a kid by the name of Babe Adams, into the box. And the Babe did all right.

He walked Cobb in the first inning and Tyrus scored on a clean hit by Jim Delahanty, but that was all the Bengals could do with the kid's slants all afternoon. There was only one other inning in which the Tigers threatened at all, the fifth. Davey Jones was on base and the Georgia Peach was at bat. The Babe pitched carefully, too carefully, and Ty tagged one. It was a beauty, a terrific clout to the farthest reaches of the center field wall. But with the crack of the bat, Pittsburgh's center fielder Tommy Leach was off like a hare—and with that last split-second desperation he leaped and the ball struck the webbing of his glove—and held. Instead of smacking a possible game-turning home run, the Peach was just another out and Adams

116

breezed the rest of the way while his teammates blasted Tiger pitcher George Mullin for four runs and the ball game. It looked like another bleak series for Hugh Jennings, Ty Cobb and Company. They had played eleven World Series games and out of the eleven all they had been able to salvage was an unsatisfactory tie game and one solitary, lonely victory.

The rookie Babe Adams, who had won only twelve and lost three in the regular season, did it in the first game. Pirate star pitcher Howard Camnitz took to the hill in the second and it looked like he was going to carry on the tradition, almost before he got to the mound. All Pittsburgh did in its first licks was to score two solid runs.

But the Tigers, goaded by the shadow of disgrace, suddenly came to life. First they scored two to tie up the game, then two more to take the lead. At this point in the proceedings the Georgia Peach took a hand in the scoring, a personal hand. Cobb was on third base, comfortably perched, as if he were the most comfortable man in the ball park, perfectly relaxed and perfectly at peace with himself, as if there were no other place he'd rather be. Then, with George Moriarty at the plate and relief pitcher Vic Willis winding up on the mound for the Pirates, the Peach suddenly lit out and streaked for home. Willis wasn't taken completely by surprise. Nor was anybody else in the stands. For all the seeming disinterest of Cobb, there was no telling when he would make a dash for the extra base. And there he was, streaking for that extra base—and a run to boot. Quickly, Willis snapped the ball to the plate. Cobb hit the dirt, his steel spikes flashing. Catcher Gibson put the ball on him. Too late. The Peach had stolen home and a thunderous shout of approval and acclamation shook the stands.

The Pirates had seen some pretty good base running in their own league. That all-time great Hans Wagner, playing shortstop for the club, was no slouch at stealing bases. But they had never seen anything like the Georgia Jewel before.

In a way, this series was one of those personal duels, a duel between the Corsair Wagner and the Tiger Cobb. Each man had led his league perennially in hitting—and this was the one time the two batting champs of any one year met in the big classic. And the Flying Dutchman was certainly in Cobb's class on the base paths. Public interest was high on the outcome of this personal clash, almost as high as it was on the fight for the World's Championship itself, and Tyrus had scored first with his beautifully executed theft of home.

The applause rocked the stands in tribute to the boy from Georgia. The fans in the Smoky City are like fans everywhere. They will stand up and cheer a good play, a good catch, a mighty swat, a brilliant run, whoever the player is who makes it. Hans Wagner approved, too, even if the Peach was stealing some of his glory, and in his own home town ball park. Wagner could afford to approve.

No all-time team can be complete without the Dutchman at shortstop. Few men have left a base-ball record behind them which can begin to compete with the record of the glorious Wagner. It wasn't only the long string of batting championships which he compiled, or his brilliance in the field and in running the bases. It was his heart as well, a big, generous heart and a staunch and brave one, too. He had an opportunity to demonstrate the heart and the spirit in which he played the game during that 1909 classic. And it was Ty Cobb who presented him with the opportunity.

Ty was on first base and, as usual, he was itching to be on the move. He was also itching to do a little tangling with that man playing the shortfield, Hans Wagner himself. The Dutchman had earned Cobb's respect before they actually met on the playing field. The boy from Georgia knew all about him, knew his record almost as well as he knew his own. As a matter of fact, Wagner was really one of the very few men in baseball for whom the petulant Cobb did have any real respect. That gave him all the more reason to see the stuff he was really made of.

"Hey!" he shouted out to the Dutchman. Cobb cupped his hands. "Hey! Kraut-head! Watch me, Kraut-head! I'm going down! I'm coming down on the next pitch!"

And he did!

But this time it was catcher Gibson who threw the ball, a strike across the diamond, and the "Kraut-head" came down with the ball hard—flush on the Peach's mouth.

"Out!" signaled the umpire.

He was out all right, and almost out of the game. There was a deep gash on the Georgian's lips and he wasn't going to be able to eat too comfortably for the next couple of days, but Ty Cobb just picked himself out of the dust, brushed his uniform, looked at the Dutchman quizzically—not without some admiration—and walked back to the Tiger bench.

There were no words between the two great stars and Cobb never uttered a syllable in protest against "unnecessary roughness." Wagner played the game the way Cobb played the game and the Peach recognized it that way. Give and take. That was his rule, and if it was good enough for him it was certainly good enough for the Flying Dutchman. It was too bad for baseball that those two great ones met for so very short a time on the diamond battlefields.

The Pirates never recovered from that Cobb steal of home and the Tigers finally had their first victory over the Pirates. Hope, like the eternal flame, bloomed in the camp of the Bengals.

"It's just as easy winning them as losing them," said Tiger manager Jennings. "Now let's go out and take the rest."

The Pirates had another notion of the way things should be run and in the third game of the series promptly scored six runs to let Detroit know how they felt about matters. The Tigers rallied. They scored four times, Cobb contributing a single to bring Detroit back into the game. In the ninth a Cobb smash had the Pittsburgh bench in a dither, a smash which all but sent the game into extra innings.

The Corsairs had made it eight to four in their half of the ninth but again the Tiger found its teeth and there were Davey Jones and Donie Bush on the bases when the hard-hitting Georgian stepped up to bat. He watched one go by, then laced into the second offering and the ball shot like a bolt for the stands. This time there wasn't a man on the Pirate squad fast enough to catch up with it. The only man who could possibly catch it was someone sitting or standing in that overflow crowd which jammed Bennett Field, for that's where the ball landed.

It should have been a home run. It would have been a home run any day in the regulation season. But it had landed among the spectators in the overflow section and that made it an automatic double. Two runs scored. Ty was on second and the tying run at the plate. But there he remained and the Pirates won it eight to six. It was two games for Pittsburgh, one for the Bengals.

The Tiger came back snarling and took the fourth game of the series five to nothing. It was the first win for Detroit of a World Series game in their home town and Ty Cobb had contributed a double to the merrymaking. The town went wild.

Pirate pitcher Babe Adams cooled them off in the

121

fifth game. Not without a struggle, however, and in the sixth game the Tigers put on one of the most thrilling exhibitions ever witnessed in a fall classic.

Three times in the first inning of that game a Corsair scampered across home plate with a run for Pittsburgh and Detroit was ready to go into deep mourning for its valiant ball club. But this year the Tiger was coming back. The Bengal got one run back in their half of the first, tied it up in the fourth, went one run to the good in the fifth. The sixth and most important run of the game came in the sixth inning, Ty Cobb again coming to the rescue with a beautiful two-base hit to score Davey Jones from second.

The Tigers needed that run. The Pirates came to bat with blood in their eyes for the ninth, and in one of the roughest, toughest innings in the history of the classic they almost turned the tide of the battle.

Dots Miller and Bill Abstein came up with a couple of singles. Wilson tried to push the potential tying runs into scoring position with a sacrifice bunt. The sacrifice worked, Miller and Abstein advancing a base each, but when Wilson crashed into the Tiger first baseman Tom Jones the storm was on. Schmidt fielded Wilson's bunt cleanly and cleanly pegged it down to Jones, but the ball, Wilson and the first baseman got to first base almost simultaneously and the impact sent both ballplayers sprawling. Wilson was able to get up to his feet but not Tom Jones. Jones was carried off the field in a stretcher. That was bad enough. What made the Tigers madder was that Miller had scored on the play.

But the Corsairs weren't playing patsy either. With just one needed to tie it up, Abstein came dashing for home plate and his spikes were high, too high. Pitcher Mullin, however, was not caught napping, and neither was Charlie Schmidt. George pitched a strike and Charlie put the tag on the man for the out, but there was a fearful crash and the two players tangled. They went at each other and there would have been one of those real, earnest, bloody scraps if there weren't calmer heads and hands in the field to pull them apart.

Nor was that the end of hostilities that afternoon. With Eddie Abbaticcio at bat, Wilson began to dance off second. George Mullin snapped a third strike across the plate and Wilson was off for third. This time it was Moriarty who put the ball on the runner, this time for the third out and for the third victory in the World Series for the Detroit Tigers. But this time, too, it was Moriarty who took the spiking and the benches emptied as the Bengals and the Corsairs went for each other.

It took the police to clear the ball field that day.

There were more fireworks in the seventh and final game of that tremendous seesaw of a World Series. Wild Bill Donovan started things right off in the very first inning by plunking Bobbie Byrne in the ribs. This was enough to get the kettle going again and it soon came to a boil. Byrne went to second on a sacrifice. That was all right. But then he lit out for third and with his spikes first. Again it was Moriarty who took the ball and put it on the runner and this time it was the runner who couldn't get up to his feet. This time it was the runner who was carried off the field. The near riot was on again and it took a good deal of talk and a lot more body blocking to get the players back into the game they were supposed to be playing.

Play did resume, finally. But the violence did not end there, at least it did not end on the part of the Pirates. Except this time they said it and did it with their bats. They pushed eight runs across the plate while Babe Adams, the same Babe who had licked the Tigers twice before, did it again. Only this time he laid it on thick. The Bengal was evidently played out. He couldn't score a single, solitary run in the entire nine innings.

The Tigers had gone down to defeat again in the World Series classic, but for once it was with a sense of glory. They had tussled with one of the greatest teams in the history of baseball and had made them fight to the wire for the championship. Hughie Jennings and Detroit might well have been proud of their boys, and they were. They played hard for their city and their heads were bloody but unbowed in defeat. It was the best World Series exhibition by a Tiger team and there was some poetic justice to the exhibition. This 1909 team was the last club Jennings would pilot to an American League flag. It was also the last pennant-winning team Detroit could boast for many years to come.

Unfortunately for all of baseball, it was also the last World Series in which that greatest of all ballplayers, Ty Cobb, would participate. That is the way it is with baseball. A star will play for years and years, burning up the league with his hitting, his fielding or his pitching, and yet never once get into the great classic. The Big Train, Walter Johnson, got to it only in the twilight of his career. There are those who were less fortunate than even the all-time great pitcher. Ty Cobb helped win three flags, played in three World Series. Yet he deserved better. The greatest of all championships—the World Series Championship—eluded him, was never his during all his glorious career.

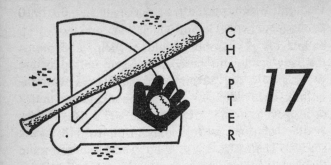

Following their three quick pennants in 1907, 1908 and 1909, the Detroit Tigers were not destined to give the automobile city another pennant for a full twenty-five years. It wasn't until 1934 when the fiery Mickey Cochrane came to manage the Bengals, when the Tigers had Charlie Gehringer, Hank Greenberg and Goose Goslin on their squad, when Schoolboy Rowe, Tommy Bridges and Hot Potato Hamlin were pitching for them, that Detroit brought another flag home to wave in the breezes of Navin Field. Ty Cobb was then only a memory to the club, and maybe an inspiration. He was more than that, even in the many lean years between the Bengal pennants.

In 1909 he had won the batting crown with a tremendous average of .377. Perhaps Detroit was going nowhere in particular in the year 1910—not with Connie Mack's gang of up-and-coming youngsters tearing the league apart and winning the flag by a mere fourteen and a half games, but the

Georgia Peach picked up in the spring of 1910 from where he had left off the year before.

The fans heckled him unmercifully. They came out to see him in droves; they loved to watch him at the plate, thrilling to the speed and the brilliance with which he caught up with that almost impossible liner screaming for the fences. They shook their park with their applause for his daring on the base paths; still they maligned him from the comparative safety of their seats in the grandstands and the bleachers.

Nor was the relationship between the Peach and his teammates much better than it had been when he broke into the line-up as a cocky rookie. The hazing was done and over with but you would have to go far and listen hard to catch one faint phrase that was even remotely friendly to the belligerent star of the Detroit Tigers. Maybe one of the reasons the Bengals were no real opposition to the Philadelphia Athletics was the internal bickering. Or perhaps it was the way Connie's boy's were taking the rest of the league over that made for all the internal squabbles in the Detroit Club. Whichever was the case, and both are probably true, Ty Cobb never did anything to make for peace among his teammates. He had been embittered early and he wasn't a man to forget easily all the indignities that had been heaped on him. The Cobb came in for his share of the fighting which flared up all season—and there was one fight with Billie Evans under the stands, after a game, which was a humdinger.

The story of the Georgia Peach in baseball is the story of one man's continual struggle to assert himself, to be recognized for what he was worth, to be duly accredited with his ability, his skill and his value. Sometimes that fight took the form of an out-and-out brawl. Sometimes it took a more subtle form. The way in which they tried to steal the Georgian's well-earned batting crown from him in 1910 might be considered subtle. More plainly, it must be considered downright dishonest.

There were two men in the race for the 1910 batting title—Larry Lajoie, the all-American star who was playing ball for Cleveland, and, of course, Tyrus Raymond Cobb. Right from the first crack of the bat of the season, the two men were at it. Lajoie, the French-Canadian ex-cab driver, had been the batting champion in 1901, 1903, and 1904. He was a veteran and, unlike Cobb, there wasn't anyone in baseball who had anything but the best to say of the ex-batting champion. On the contrary, there wasn't a ballplayer or a fan in the country, except perhaps in Detroit, who wasn't pulling for Larry Lajoie to beat out the Georgian in the race for the American League batting crown. And even in Detroit, and among his own teammates, there were many who preferred to see the Peach taken down a step.

There was a tremendous amount of added interest that year, too, introduced by the Chalmers Automobile Company.

"We will present to the batting champions in both the American League and the National

League," they announced to the press at the beginning of the season, "in recognition of their ability and of their championship performance, a Chalmers car."

It gave the Chalmers Company a good bit of publicity. It also gave a bit of an impetus to the race for the baseball honors of the year. Ballplayers and fans alike were more keenly aware of the race for batting honors than they had ever been before, while the nip-and-tuck affair Cobb and Lajoie were making of the fight for the crown, and the automobile, added fuel to the fires of their interest.

Right down to the last day it went—and with Connie Mack's Philadelphians making a runaway of it in the American League, everybody was more excited about the batting championship than about the outcome of the games themselves.

Ty Cobb ended his year's campaigning with a smashing .385, bettering his 1909 mark of .376 by .009 percentage points. He was out of the line-up for the last game of the season, and with Larry Lajoie considerably behind, it looked for certain that Cobb had made it—run a string of four batting championships in a row and won the Chalmers car to boot. There was still that outside chance for Lajoie. There always is that outside chance in baseball. But even with Cleveland slated for a double-header with the St. Louis Browns in its final day of the season, no one—certainly none of the most rabid of Lajoie well-wishers—could hope for very much.

They didn't reckon, however, with a bit of misguided loyalty, a touch of chicanery and some of the weirdest events in the history of baseball.

The first time Lajoie came to bat on that last day of regulation play baseball in 1910 he whacked out a tremendous drive which might have been a homer in these days of the shorter fences. It was a mighty swat but Brownie outfielder Hub Northern went after it and it looked like he had it until suddenly he turned his face and lost the ball. Lajoie was standing on third base with a triple before the ball was gotten back to the infield.

The stands had let out a mighty roar of approval at the crack of the bat and it didn't let up its roaring throughout the afternoon. They wanted Lajoie to get that car—and with his first trip to the plate he had raised high the hopes that sparkled timidly in all the fans assembled that afternoon.

Northern had lost the ball in the sun and the Larruping Larry had made a gain, however slight, on the league-leading Cobb. There was one more clean hit Lajoie got that long afternoon, a clean single. The rest of the story is rather ghoulish.

Lajoie was at bat and Red Corriden, who was then a rookie third baseman for the Browns, turned to his manager Jack O'Connor for instructions.

"Play him deep," ordered O'Connor.

Even the rookie knew that the veteran Lajoie had slowed down on his feet and he looked questioningly at his manager.

"On the grass," ordered O'Connor.

Corriden played deep.

"You're boss," he said but he knew that the grass was no place to play Lajoie—that is, if you wanted to get the putout on him, and he was right.

Six times that afternoon Larry Lajoie bunted and six times he got to first base before the ball.

"Let me play close," Corriden asked.

"On the grass," ordered O'Connor.

And after every bunt Lajoie executed, Harry Howell, pitching and coaching for the St. Louis Club, made a trip to the press box to ask how those bunts were being scored.

The crowd, of course, went delirious with enthusiasm. Eight out of eight for Lajoie and they were sure that the popular Larry had nosed out the less popular Ty Cobb.

And that's how practically every sport sheet in the country saw it. One paper had Lajoie ahead of the Georgian by fully three points. Others were less generous, but one way or another they managed to crown Lajoie batting champion of the American League. The *Sporting News,* one of the few supporters of Cobb, gave it to the Peach by .38415 to .38411.

Officially, the great Cobb was awarded the batting crown by a full point and Ban Johnson—that tempestuous leader of the American League—made an investigation of the whole affair which didn't have too sweet a smell about it, and which threatened nothing good for baseball and the baseball world.

Red Corriden was cleared. He had taken orders and a ballplayer is supposed to take orders, but O'Connor and Howell were both dropped by the St. Louis Browns.

The Chalmers Company circumnavigated the entire mess by awarding cars to both Lajoie and Cobb, but no one else tried to take a batting crown away from the Georgian ever again—that is, by any means that might be considered foul. The only way to beat Tyrus out of his title was by banging out more hits and banging them out more often.

In 1910 Tyrus Raymond Cobb fashioned himself a fancy .385 at the bat. In 1911, 1912, 1913— in 1921 and 1922—the great Georgia Peach would do better, a lot better.

There never was a batsman in organized ball— American League, National League, any league— who could approach the skill, the know-how, the sheer batting intelligence of the magnificent Georgia Peach.

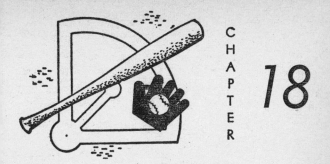

"MY BEST years as a ballplayer?" said Ty Cobb.

There's always someone who sends in the query.

"I guess," answered Ty, "maybe the best years I ever played were 1911, 1912 and 1913."

It's just as hard for the Georgia Peach to tab any special season as his greatest, as it is for the most astute students and historians of the game. There can be no denying, however, that in 1911 the Peach was playing as brilliantly as any man could possibly hope to play the game on the diamond.

The Tigers came in a hopeless second to the high-riding Philadelphia Athletics who won the flag by thirteen and a half games, but there was nothing hopeless about the way Ty Cobb burned up the league with his bat and romped around the bases as if the game had been invented especially for the Georgian.

For the third time in his career he led the American loop with eighty-three stolen bases. He scored the greatest number of runs for the third straight year with one hundred and forty-seven of them. For the fourth time he came in with the most hits in the league with two hundred and forty-eight. And for the second time he banged out the most doubles and triples—forty-seven two-baggers and twenty-four for three bases. The league leadership in batting percentage was another one of those down-to-the-wire affairs.

Shoeless Joe Jackson, the sensational ballplayer from South Carolina who was to end up unhappily with the Black Sox scandal of the 1919 World Series, was playing his first full year with the Cleveland Club in 1911. In 1910 Shoeless had come up late and gotten into only twenty games, but in those twenty games he had banged out a batting percentage of .387 and Tyrus had gotten a good glimpse of him.

"I like the way you handle that bat," he had said to the youngster.

That was right friendly of Cobb, as friendly as he would get on the playing field.

Shoeless Joe looked at him with the reverence of a rookie for a man who had already attained stardom on the diamond.

"I do my best, Mr. Cobb."

"You're doing all right."

"Thank you, Mr. Cobb."

Ty, fierce competitor that he was, nevertheless appreciated a natural player when he saw one. For all his desire to be Number One, very often he took a younger batter in hand and taught him a few tricks at the plate. Even Ted Williams, that great hitter of the Boston Red Sox, cornered the great Georgian in the ball park one day and held him for hours after the park had been cleared, in order to get some pointers on how to bat them out to where they couldn't be reached. And Cobb was more than a willing teacher. He was an eager and skillful teacher.

It bothered the Peach, that the "Williams shift" was taking hit after hit away from the temperamental Ted. Cobb got hold of a close friend of the Red Soxer and bent his ear with advice for the Boston outfielder, then sat down and wrote him a two-page letter on how to hit them to left field. Everybody who has followed the story of Williams knows that the moment he got up to bat, his whole opposition—infield and outfield—shifted to right.

The story is that on the day Ted Williams got that letter from the great Cobb he got four hits, a homer, a couple of doubles and a single, and every one of the blasts went left of second base.

The Red Soxer developed even greater prowess than he had already exhibited, and much of the credit had to go to the Georgian who knew more about batting than any man in baseball. Nor was Williams the first improved batter because of Cobb's instruction. But that part of the story comes later.

That afternoon he talked to Shoeless Joe, telling him that he was doing all right. He was more frank and open with some of the boys on the Bengal squad.

"That Jackson fellow is going to become one of the greatest hitters in the game," he said.

Coming from Ty Cobb, this was more than a prophecy. It was a warning to all American League pitchers that they were to remember for nine good years.

And it was Shoeless Joe Jackson who threatened to take the league's batting championship in 1911. As a matter of fact, the boy who had come up from the cotton mills of South Carolina, where he had been an ordinary hand, was leading the American League by fully nineteen points with only twelve games left to the season. But six of those games were to be played between the Tigers and the Naps, and even though they were being played in Jackson's own back yard, so to speak, the Cleveland ball park, there was the psychological attack of Ty Cobb's which was to stalk between him and the batting championship.

"I won't talk to him," said Cobb.

" 'Lo, Mr. Cobb," said the still revering Shoeless.

The Peach just passed him by.

Joe Jackson figured Ty hadn't heard him and the next time they met he repeated, "How are things, Mr. Cobb?"

Ty Cobb didn't even look at him.

This time Shoeless Joe knew that Ty had heard him and he was puzzled.

I didn't do anything wrong, he thought to himself.

They had to pass each other as one team came in from the field and the other went out to take up its positions.

"Mr. Cobb," called Shoeless, timidly.

Ty was deaf.

And Shoeless worried about it and his batting average fell off, as the master-minding Ty Cobb's mounted.

The Georgian was sure that his psychological trick had turned the tide. He still liked the boy from South Carolina, as much as he could like a ballplayer, but he had wanted to upset him—and he did.

However, it is pretty much the consensus of opinion among baseball writers that Cobb didn't need that trick at all. This was the year Ty set a record by hitting safely in forty-one straight games and ended his season with an absolutely astounding batting average of .420, a good twelve points better than the brilliant .408 of the rookie Jackson. This .420 average stood for thirteen years until, in 1924, the magnificent Rogers Hornsby batted .424 for St. Louis. And only one other man has reached that mark in either league. George Sisler did it for the Browns in 1922.

Jackson was a great hitter. It was one of his misfortunes that he was batting them out when Ty Cobb was in his prime, and Ty Cobb's prime lasted a very long time.

Once in a while a man would turn up and hold the great Cobb at bay for a while. But only for a while. Then, as if the pitcher had lost all his stuff, the Tyrus would start banging him around —and to every part of the diamond.

The Georgian was taking his licks, and even while he was going down swinging he was studying the pitcher, studying his pitches. Then from the bench he continued to watch the hurler as he tossed them into the plate.

The pitcher's fast one had a peculiar hook. The pitcher's curve broke at the last split second. The Georgian adjusted his batting stance, moved up in the batter's box or back in it, as his findings dictated. After this little bit of scientific investigation, the pitcher was just another cousin to the astounding Peach.

When Walter Johnson came up into the big leagues, he poured them into the plate so fast that the batters were swinging with the ball already in the catcher's mitt.

"You can't hit them if you can't see them," said Ty Cobb.

That's been said many times since about a number of the fast boys who came up into the big-time company. It was never truer than the first time it was said, and then by Cobb after facing the Big Train for the first time in his career.

But Ty Cobb learned how to hit Johnson, the way he learned to hit against everyone else, and he banged Johnson for a better than .300 lifetime average.

"He's got the fastest pitch I ever saw," said Ty

Cobb, but he discovered the Big Train's weakness, and that was all he needed to discover.

Ty crowded the plate. No one has ever hugged the plate more tightly. They threw at his head to move him out of there. They probably threw more bean balls at Ty Cobb than any player who ever stepped up to home plate with a bat. But there was never a man in baseball who was up to the plate more often and was hit less. The Georgian practiced the bunt, the precise way in which to hit the ball to the spot vacated for the fraction of a second. He also practiced how to get away from that inside pitch. And the pitchers knew it, too. Maybe Walter Johnson didn't know it. However, even if he did, the Big Train never threw a "duster." His heart was too big for it.

It was this big heart which was Ty Cobb's discovery. He knew that the Big Train would never intentionally throw one at his head. He also knew that Johnson worried a lot about even the possibility of hitting a batter. This was more than enough for the astute Peach, and whenever he came to bat against the speedball artist he crowded that plate more than ever.

The result: Johnson kept pitching them outside, and while Cobb could hit anything inside or outside, low, high or just in the middle, that added bit of information that Walter would send the ball on the outside was enough for Cobb. He hit the Big Train as well as he hit anybody else, something of which very few batters in the league could boast.

Of course, this does not detract from the superb

record of the great Walter Johnson. Ty Cobb could really hit. Fourteen times in his career he batted out five for five and better. Against Philadelphia in a six-game series played in three double-headers, the Peach hammered out two homers, three triples, three doubles and ten ordinary singles for eighteen out of twenty-seven. Against St. Louis he hammered out five home runs in two days, and there were a couple more which just missed the fence by inches. He was a terror to every pitcher who ever threw a ball in his direction, and no wonder. He could punch a ball in any direction he chose. He could smack the apple out to any part of the outfield—and over the fence, if there was sufficient need for it. He was a nice guy to have on your own side, but for the opposition he was one continuous headache. He even introduced the business of taking a full swing at the ball just to foul it off. Eddie Stanky, among others, was mighty good at it but could have taken lessons from Ty Cobb in this skill. The Peach also introduced the business of swinging hard at the first pitch only to swing the surprise bunt on the next, or vice versa.

In 1911, when the most valuable player award was instituted by the same Chalmers Automobile Company—which in a small way added to the confusion of the 1910 race for the batting championship—sixty-four sports writers voted and all sixty-four of them voted Tyrus Raymond Cobb the Most Valuable Player of the American League in the season of 1911.

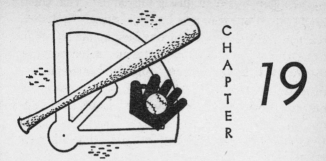

PERHAPS the most fantastic rhubarb in the history of the baseball diamond occurred in 1912. Ty Cobb, of course, was in the middle of it. As a matter of fact, it was the Georgia Peach who started the whole rumpus.

Cobb had come in for a lot of abuse from his teammates when he first broke into the game. It is also more or less a matter of record that no ball-player ever suffered more abuse at the hands of the fans. And the controversies the Georgian raised continuously in the press fed the flames of the fans' antagonisms. No matter what Ty Cobb did, at the bat or in the field, he was sure to be the target of the boys sitting in the stands.

Ty Cobb took most of what the fans gave him in much the same manner that he took what the Bengals gave him in 1905 and 1906. He didn't throw any pop bottles back into the bleachers but his tongue was as sharp as anyone else's. There was one day, however, when the Peach thought one of the fans had gone just a bit too far. That's when the fireworks started.

It was May 15, Detroit was playing the New York Club in their Highlander Park and a fellow by the name of Lucker, a minor political henchman, was giving Ty Cobb the razzberry.

Ty looked up at the offender, made sure of his identity.

"You mouth's too big for you, boy!" he cautioned.

But the misguided fan was just beginning to warm up and he continued his tirade more vehemently.

"You'd better cut it out!" warned Cobb, more sharply.

But the fan was having a good time, if the Tiger wasn't, and he hurled a few more prize epithets at the Georgian.

Ty issued one more warning.

"I guess there's only one thing that'll shut you up!" he shouted.

But the fan behind the wooden railings felt pretty secure with the barrier between him and the fuming Peach. He let go again with a string of abusive phrases and that was just about too much for anybody to take. The tempestuous Peach was at him.

Over the railing he leaped, singled out the foul-mouthed culprit and let him have it.

Jumping over the rails, of course, and beating up a spectator is strictly forbidden in baseball, and the petulant Peach was immediately thumbed out of the game by the umpire.

Ban Johnson, American League chief, was in the stands that afternoon, too. He saw the whole dramatic incident, exactly as it happened. He didn't have to wait too long for the umpire's report and immediately suspended the Georgian for an indefinite period.

The Detroit squad, which was never too fond of the Peach, should have been pleased with the suspension. For once the Georgian had been set down, and set down properly.

But no one playing with the Tigers said, "He got what was coming to him."

There wasn't a Bengal who said, "It's about time someone took the guy down a peg or two."

On the contrary, every active player on the club, without exception, rose up in defense of the Peach. An indignation meeting was held and unanimously the Tigers voted the most drastic, the most dramatic action taken collectively by a team in the history of the sport. The Detroit Tigers voted to go on strike and to stay on strike till Ty Cobb was reinstated.

"Feeling Mr. Cobb is being done an injustice," they wired the president of the league Ban Johnson, "by your action in suspending him we, the undersigned, refuse to play in another game after today until such action is adjusted to our satisfaction. He was fully justified in his action, as no one could stand such vile and personal abuse from anyone. We want him reinstated for tomorrow's game, May 18, or there will be no game. If players cannot have protection, we must protect ourselves."

And every player on the squad, with the exception of Ty Cobb himself, signed that telegram to the head office of the league.

Why the Detroit ball team took such a militant stand, despite their personal feeling about the Georgian, is one of those peculiar mysteries of human behavior. Most likely the reasons for this earnest, aggressive defense of a ballplayer can be found in the words of the wire they sent Ban Johnson.

For one, the Bengals knew the value of Cobb to the team, whatever else they felt about him. Without Cobb, the team which was already floundering in the first months of the new season would simply plummet to the very bottom of the league. Second —and certainly no less important—baseball players in every club in the leagues, minor or major, were just about fed up with the filth they had to take from the fans in the stands. And filth is not too harsh a word to use for some of the language too many of the spectators hurled at the boys on the diamond.

For once the ballplayers took their stand. They didn't want the fans shut up. They *wanted* the fans to speak up, to shout out their approval as well as their disapproval. The noise the fans make is part of the game, an exciting, dramatic part of the game. But they wanted the obscenity cut out. They wanted to stop the personal references to any man unable to defend himself. They wanted Ty Cobb exonerated as an indication that the league would support the player against the excessive language of the spectator. They certainly didn't want the fans to use the suspension as an added excuse and protection for further and intensified abuse from the ugly spectators who managed to degrade the rest of baseball's fandom.

But Ban Johnson, one of the toughest fighters who ever held a front office job in baseball, wasn't easily frightened. When he suspended a player that suspension held, and it would hold no matter what.

"The suspension has not been lifted," he announced to the press. "Cobb will not be seen in the Detroit line-up today, nor will he be seen in it for some time to come."

And everybody knew that Johnson was as good as his word. Hughie Jennings knew it and he wired Frank Navin back in Detroit, "What shall we do?"

Frank Navin knew it and he wired back to Jennings, "If the team refuses to go out on the field, get a team that will."

The league rules—and Frank Navin knew them, too—placed a neat fine of five thousand dollars a day on a club that didn't show up for a scheduled game. More than that, there was the possibility of the loss of his franchise. Detroit could be thrown out of the league as easily as that. Hughie Jennings knew that, too. And so did Cobb.

As a matter of record, Cobb himself urged the players to think it over before they sent the telegram threatening their strike. So did Ee-yah Jennings. It didn't help. The ball club was really up in arms.

So, too, according to the rumors which came a dime a dozen that day in May of 1912, were the other clubs around the league. The Philadelphia

Athletics, whom the Tigers were scheduled to play on the day they had threatened to strike, according to one of the reports about town, had informed Connie Mack that if the Bengals didn't show up at the ball park they would follow suit. Ballplayers, they believed, should stand together against the abuse of the stands.

Another rumor had it that a league meeting had been called to which every club was to send a player representative. A third report had it that there would be a general strike of all ballplayers if Cobb were not reinstated by the following Monday.

Quite a little business that stormy petrel from Georgia had started!

And the Detroit team did go on strike, just as they had threatened.

"Just as if they were freight handlers," reported *The New York Times* in a front-page story, "New England millworkers, striking longshoremen, or belonging to any of the disaffected class of craftsmen who have wage troubles, the athletes paraded off the field just before the hour for calling play—literally a walkout."

The fans looked on in awe and amazement and well they might, for such a scene had never been witnessed in a ball park before.

The Detroit players had carried out their threat but the host of rumors were just that, rumors and nothing more, and Connie Mack's boys, when the umpire called, "Play ball," trotted out to their positions.

Now five thousand dollars is a big heap of money at any time, and in 1912 it was worth a good deal more in groceries than it is worth today. Frank Navin wasn't paying a fine of five thousand dollars, not if he could help it. And certainly he wasn't risking the loss of his very, very valuable franchise.

There wasn't a regular Bengal on the Tiger's bench that afternoon, but there was a team that Hughie Jennings put together at the last minute. At least it went into the records as a team. The oldster "Deacon" Jim McGuire was there, Tiger scout and former Cleveland manager. Snow-topped Joe Sugden who had played ball with practically every club in the majors at one time or another was there. Al Travers, who was later to become a reverend and who was something of a semipro pitcher, handled the mound chores, McGarvey and McGarr, both of whom had played ball for Georgetown University, were Tigers for the day. So was Billy Maig, who had done some fighting as a lightweight and who was a better fighter than a ballplayer; Joe Harrigan who had been recommended as a ballplayer with some kind of reputation; and a Billy Feinhauser and an E. Ward, whom nobody knew at all. Even Hughie Jennings got into the game at one stage of the festivities—as a pinch-hitter.

As might have been expected, there was nothing resembling a contest in the game. Connie pitched Jack Coombs, Carrol Brown and Herb Pennock for three innings apiece, while all the Mackmen fattened up their batting averages at the expense of the lionhearted Al Travers, who was hired for twenty-five dollars and got a twenty-five dollar bonus for sticking out the slaughter. The rest of the semipros, amateurs and what-have-you's collected ten dollars each for their labors, and judging from the reaction of the fans they all deserved some sort of bonus from the Detroit Club. And that includes the striking Detroit players as well, because instead of driving off in the taxis which had been waiting for them at the park exit, they had all turned around, bought tickets and watched the game from all over the stands.

"It's a circus," said Donie Bush. "I sure am glad I came."

"I wouldn't have missed it for a minute," said the fiery Jim Delahanty.

Of course it was a circus. The Athletics romped all over the field. Eddie Collins stole five bases and smacked out four hits. McInnis and Strunk got four hits each, too. The "Detroit Tigers" were simply swamped twenty-four to two.

Meanwhile the kettle was boiling. Joe Wood, Boston Red Sox pitcher, Harry Lord, captain of the Chicago White Sox, and many other ballplayers around the league were getting wires from the Tigers asking for support by way of action of the ballplayers.

The center of the storm, Ty Cobb, issued a statement:

"Ban Johnson has always believed himself to be

infallible. He suspends a man first and investigates afterward. It should be the reverse."

Connie Mack, in response to a request for his views, said,

"I know from my own experience as a ballplayer that one gets little sympathy from the grandstand and far less from the bleachers and some of the things a big-league player is forced to listen to can make one's blood boil in resentment. Yet I think they can adopt more telling methods than by going into the spectators' reservations and dealing out summary punishment."

It was a wise statement but the players wanted action, not words.

"League presidents and managers have to listen to players sometimes," said Cobb, "and this is a good chance."

And the presidents and the managers did listen, and so did Ban Johnson.

The next game with Philadelphia was postponed and the big Ban came east from Cincinnati, leaving a banquet at which he was the guest of honor immediately on receiving a telegram from Frank Navin earnestly requesting a meeting in the City of Brotherly Love.

"I am amazed at the attitude of Cobb and his teammates," he told reporters.

"We will fight it out, and we are right," declared the aggressive Peach. "Johnson will see the light and see it hard. He is not the man to ignore a fair deal—and we have one coming."

There was a big confab, there were a lot of big

confabs. Ban Johnson, Frank Navin, Hugh Jennings, Connie Mack, James McAleer of the Boston Red Sox, Frank Farrell of the New York Yankees, Ty Cobb and all the rest of the Bengals—and it was Ty Cobb who urged the boys to go back into the game.

"It's the thing to do," he said. "It's the thing to do for all of us, and for baseball."

The boys went back—and maybe there wasn't too much heart in their decision, for all they got in the next game they played were two hits. Of course they were hitting against Walter Johnson, Washington's Big Train, and that must be taken into consideration. Strangely enough, they won that game two to nothing, and it was George Mullin who pitched that brilliant shutout for Detroit that first afternoon after the only strike of its kind in baseball.

Ty Cobb, as might have been expected, was reinstated after a ten-day suspension and a fifty-dollar fine. As for the rest of the squad, they had their one day of fun watching the Detroit "pick-up team" chasing the ball all over the lot, but Ban Johnson slapped them each down with a hundred-dollar fine. A curious turn of justice.

As for the fans, there was one incident later on in the season which was laid directly to the incident which took place in Highlander Park. It was in Detroit and the Peach was driving with his wife when three hoodlums jumped on the running board of his car and began to slash at Cobb with ugly knives. The Georgian was never one to run away from a fight and he wasn't running away from this one. He stopped the motor, got out of the car and took on all three of the thugs. It wasn't Cobb who quit. It was the mugs.

Ty was pretty badly cut up and needed a good bit of bandaging. He reported the story to the police but they never caught up with the hoodlums. It was never really proved but the general opinion was that somebody hadn't forgotten the beating administered by the Georgian to the fan in Highlander Park.

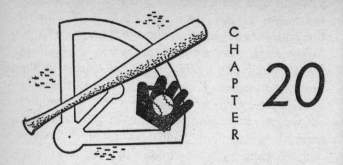

CHAPTER 20

THERE was a lot of noise in 1912, columns and columns about Ty Cobb and the Detroit Tigers, but it was all about the incident in the stands and the strike that developed out of it. Except for the automobile city, there wasn't much to say about Hughie Jennings' squad of ball players, and in their home town all the speeches, all the newsprint, all that could be said of the Bengals couldn't be added to the credit column. Jennings had given Detroit three pennant winners. In 1910 and 1911 the Tigers had come in a fighting second. In 1912 the team fell apart and landed deep in the second division. As a matter of fact, the club had all it could do to beat out the seventh place St. Louis Browns for the sixth notch in the final standings.

Ty Cobb, however, just kept rolling along. Shoeless Joe gave him another tough battle and wound up with a magnificent .395 in his second year in the big time. It wasn't enough. The irrepressible

Cobb banged out a terrific average of .410, leading the league in hits again, for the fifth time, with two hundred and twenty-seven.

The Peach was a hard man to catch. Again in 1913 he left Shoeless Joe Jackson behind in the race for the batting crown, coming up that year with a batting mark of .390.

"I just can't win," complained Shoeless Joe, wistfully.

Cobb was a tough man to beat.

New names were coming up in the baseball headlines. Rube Marquard made good his manager John McGraw's promise and hurled nineteen straight wins for the Giants. There was the great Red Sox outfield of Tris Speaker (the admirable Spoke), Harry Hooper and Duffy Lewis. Claude Hendrix was pitching them for Pittsburgh and Jim Thorpe, that greatest of all athletes, made his appearance in major league ball. Heinie Zimmerman was playing with the Cubs and batting away up in the .370's. Jake Daubert was playing with the Brooklyn Dodgers and Grover Cleveland Alexander came up with the Philadelphia National League Club to win thirty-three games in a season, sixteen of them shutouts. George Herman Ruth, the Babe himself, was the American League's leading pitcher (for 1915) hurling eighteen wins for the Bosox against six losses. In the 1916 World Series the Bambino pitched thirteen scoreless innings to beat Sherry Smith and the Brooklyn Dodgers in a fourteen-innings game by the score of two to one.

Stars were popping up all over the major league circuits but the Georgia Peach, minding his own business, kept moving at the head of the flock.

In 1914, despite a broken rib which he had picked up in a knock-down-drag-'em-out fight, and despite a broken thumb, Cobb won his eighth batting championship in a row with a big .368 average. In 1915 he won it again, this time with a .369 mark. It was this year, too, that Ty Cobb set the league on its ear with a clean steal of ninety-six bases. That's one baseball record that wasn't likely to be broken for many, many years to come. Jackie Robinson, considered one of the most daring base runners in the game, made his biggest score with Brooklyn in 1949. His total of base thefts for the year was thirty-seven. Sam Jethroe of Boston led the National League in 1950 with thirty-five stolen bases. In 1950 the American League leader in the theft department was Dom DiMaggio with the high total of fifteen. It wasn't until Maury Wills of the Los Angeles Dodgers came along that Cobb's base-stealing records were broken. In 1962, Maury stole 104 bases. Whole teams have stolen fewer bases in a complete season than Ty Cobb did on his own. Maybe he wasn't the fastest human but there was no one who could match his speed on the diamond. And it was because of his great speed that many an old-timer, fortunate enough to see the Peach in action, called him a greater fielder than he was a hitter. Considering the Georgian's terrific batting marks, he must have been the greatest fielder that ever lived. The record will have to rest there.

The year 1915 was a heartbreaker for Jennings. The Tigers came back strong that year, won one hundred games, but were nosed out of the pennant. The Red Sox did it with one hundred and one victories. It isn't often that a hundred-game winner doesn't get into the World Series, but it happened to Hughie Jennings and his Bengals.

It was just about the closest that Ty Cobb, too, batting in his ninth consecutive hitting crown in his tenth full season with Detroit, came to appearing again in the baseball classic.

"We tried," was all he could say.

And no one can accuse Ty Cobb of ever letting up in his great efforts, wherever those efforts were called on. And all his work, incidentally, wasn't on the diamond.

On May 15, 1914, just a couple of years after another memorable May 15, the New York papers ran a couple of headlines about the Detroit star.

TY COBB BUSTS RIGHT INTO
LITERARY GAME
*   *   *
TY COBB SCORES SUCCESS
AS ORATOR
*   *   *
FAMOUS BASEBALL PLAYER
MAKES DEBUT AS SPEAKER

It was at a booksellers' dinner, crowded with notables in the writing field, with speeches and letters read by such eminent figures as William Dean Howells, Ambassador Page, Woodrow Wilson, then President of the United States, and Charles Eliot of Harvard. Ty was called on to make his maiden speech, and according to reports he did proudly by himself. What's more, for all the pugnacity he exhibited on the diamond, the Georgia Peach demonstrated that he had a sense of humor second to none.

"I can't see why you want to mar my evening," he drawled, according to the newspaper accounts of the event, "by making me stand up and be uncomfortable."

But there wasn't anything uncomfortable about the man. Nothing could shake his self-confidence and his poise.

"I think I'm an accident here," he continued. "But I suppose on every occasion there's got to be a sacrifice. I'm like a young pitcher Manager Jennings sent into a game at Detroit. The first three men walked, the next up busted one—and when the smoke cleared away there were five or six runs and the bases full.

" 'Smatter? Nervous?' Mr. Jennings asked the young pitcher back at the bench.

" 'No,' said the pitcher. 'The only thing the matter with me is that I can't keep my legs from shakin', but I ain't nervous.' "

But Ty Cobb wasn't nervous and the hall boomed with approving laughter.

"I'll tell you," he said, "the only time I thought I was a Demosthenes was once when I was playing in Philadelphia. There's a city, by the way," he interpolated. "I like that dear City of Brotherly Love where they have to have three hundred cops out on the field every time we play there so we won't be mobbed. . . ."

Ty Cobb not only knew how to stand up and deliver a good talk, a humorous talk, but he also knew how to put that right word in at the right time, like a swift left jab that travels a very short distance but leaves a very telling mark.

"If instead of this ballroom," he said, drawing his speech to a close, "I only had a diamond and green grass and umpires—and the fans all calling you a lot of names that are not your own—it would be easier."

It may have been Cobb's first appearance in the speaker's box but he was certainly as much at home in it as he was when he stepped into the batter's box for the first time in the big leagues and smacked the great Chesbro's spitball for a clean two-bagger.

Nor was speaking the only extracurricular activity in which the Georgian excelled. He did a movie once and baseball almost lost the Peach to Hollywood.

Grantland Rice, that great dean of the sports world, wrote a script. *Somewhere in Georgia* he called it, and it was the story of a baseball player who upends a villain and restores order in a town,

157

in addition to seeing to it that love comes into its own. And the hero does this, despite all sorts of chicanery and villainy, by escaping from a bunch of desperados, by getting into the game in the last of the ninth inning when everything seems lost— and by belting the ball for the three winning runs which spell ruin for the bad side and happiness and everything that comes with it for the good side.

Of course, that was the way they did the movies in those days and Grantland Rice obliged. He not only gave them the story but he gave them their star ballplayer as well, the Georgia Peach, and he surprised everyone, critics as well as directors and actors, with his performance.

"For a matter of twelve years," wrote Grantland Rice in the New York *Tribune,* "Tyrus Raymond Cobb, the first citizen of Georgia, has proved that when it comes to facing pitchers he has no rival . . . he has averaged 40 points beyond all competition.

"It may have been that facing such pitchers as Walsh, Johnson, Ruth and others had acclimated Ty to facing anything under the sun, even a motion picture camera. At any rate, when Director George Ridgewell, of the Sunbeam Motion Picture Company, lined Ty up in various attitudes before the camera he was astounded at the way the star ballplayer handled the new job. . . ."

Director Ridgeway weighed in with his own opinion.

"I had an idea," he said, "that I would have to

take half my time in drilling him for various scenes. . . . But on the contrary, he seemed to have an advance hunch as to what was wanted and the picture will show that as a movie star Ty is something more than a .380 hitter."

And the critics:

"As an actor Ty Cobb is a huge success. In fact, he is so good that he shows all the others up."

Of course. Wherever Ty played he would show others up. He had to be first.

And he was the first ballplayer to build himself an independent fortune. No ballplayer had ever amassed the capital the Peach built up for himself—even while he was batting them out for the Detroit Tigers.

Very early in his career the Peach began to play around with real estate investments. They paid off. He played around with the cotton market. That paid off, too. His biggest financial maneuver, however, was his purchase of a good-sized block of Coca-Cola stock when it was selling at a little over a dollar a share. He tipped off the rest of the boys on the Bengal squad but not one of them took the tip, much to their later regret, for that stock soared up to $181 a share, paid off at one hundred and eighty-one to one, making Ty Cobb at the time the richest baseball player in the game.

The Peach was astute. He could have been a success in any field he might have entered—law, medicine, finance, a first-rater, a top man. He chose baseball and baseball history was made enormously richer for his choice.

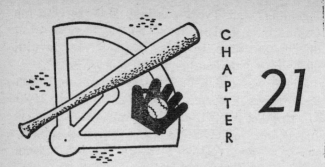

IN 1916 the Georgia Peach hammered out two hundred and one hits, scored more than any one else in the league—one hundred and thirteen times—batted .371, which was .002 better than the 1915 season, but for the first time in ten years, for the first time since 1907, the Monarch of Swat relinquished the throne which, many had thought, he would never give up.

"It had to come sometime, I guess," said the Peach, though it was hard for him to recognize the fact. "I'm glad it was Spoke who did it."

Spoke was the Gray Eagle, the Texan Tristam Speaker, known to all baseball fandom as Tris Speaker. A great outfielder, a Hall-of-Famer, the man who is always chosen—along with Babe Ruth and Ty Cobb—to patrol the all-time all-star outfield, Tris was second only to the Peach. He was what Columbia Lou Gehrig was to the Bambino, but he constantly played in the shadow of the petulant Cobb. He was up there among the ranking hitters, but Tyrus was first. He was with the leading base stealers, but Cobb was there in front of him. But once, in 1916, Speaker came in with the batting championship, hitting a lusty .386.

There was one department, however, in which the Gray Eagle soared beyond the Peach. In 1920 Tris Speaker piloted the Cleveland Indians to their first pennant in the history of the American League, and to a most decisive victory over the Dodgers for their first World Championship as well.

No one was prouder of him than Cobb, but that wasn't the way he felt in 1916.

Maybe he spent the winter brooding over the loss of his rank in batting. Maybe the more he thought about it, the more determined he was to regain that rank. Whatever the reason, the Peach came to spring training with the chip on his shoulder a bit longer than ever.

The Tigers were playing some early exhibition games with John McGraw's Giants. McGraw was just about as tough as they come in baseball. They called him the Little Napoleon and for two good reasons. First, he was one of the hardest disciplinarians in the game. The boys who played ball for the New York Giants had to toe the mark, the mark that John McGraw set for them. Second, baseball rarely witnessed a greater strategist on the field, a finer tactician in the game, a more successful manager of a baseball club. Ten times the Little Napoleon piloted his team to National League pennants, three times to the World Championship.

But in 1917 John McGraw was equally well

known for his pugnacity. No one carried a bigger chip on his shoulder. No one got into more scraps. No one went out after a scrap the way the fiery ex-Baltimore Oriole John McGraw went out for anything resembling a battle. And he imbued his men with the same kind of spirit which made them the fightingest team in the leagues.

Of course, the Detroit Tigers with their aggressive Tyrus Raymond Cobb were a little on the tough side themselves, and putting the Bengals and the Giants on the same field was like laying two hot coals side by side. You could count on fireworks.

Ty got in just in time for the game but too late for the preliminary practice session. The Peach had been a little careless about punching the mythical clock and there had been talk about it around the club and around the league. Hughie Jennings hadn't been able to do very much about getting his star to report with all the other boys and that, too, had spread around. The Giants had gotten wind of the story, like everyone else in baseball, and they were ready for the dramatic entrance of the Peach.

"Look who's here!"

"Well, what do you know? Look what's dragged in here!"

"Go on home, Cobb! This is a ball park!"

They were a tough bunch of hombres—Artie Fletcher, Eddie Roush, Benny Kauff, Fred Merkle, Jeff Tesrau, and more. Any one of them would have taken on a whole pack of wildcats at the drop of a hat.

"That's the great Ty Cobb. Don't you know?"

"Never heard of him."

"The Georgia Peach!"

"What's that?"

Cobb got red in the face but he kept his tongue.

The riding continued from the Giant bench and the Little Napoleon and all his faithful grenadiers were past masters at the art of riding.

Cobb kept the peace. This was strange for Cobb, but anyone who knew anything about the Peach knew that his serenity wasn't going to last for long.

Connie Mack used to warn his Athletics to take it easy on the Georgian.

"Rile him," he said, "and he'll smack the ball all over the place. Besides, I want you all to come out in one piece after this game is over."

Evidently this was one story the New York boys hadn't heard, and someone had to pay for it.

Ty went up to the plate swinging his bat and Jeff Tesrau hollered down to him, "I pitch 'em fast, boy! Watch out for the smoke!"

Ty just glared out at him.

Tesrau wound up, sent in a fast one, close, to drive him away from the plate.

It was too close. No one could get away from an inside pitch faster than Cobb but this one nicked him.

The Peach tossed away his bat, trotted down to first base.

"I'll take care of you the next time I'm up there," he said to the big Tesrau.

Tyrus had a way of taking care of pitchers who threw them up too close. When he was calm

163

enough he would just lay down a bunt along the first base line, just right so that the pitcher would have to head in the direction of the base and directly in the path the Peach had to run. The collision which invariably ensued would have them carrying the pitcher off the field.

Didn't Ty say, "The base paths belong to the runner?"

And he meant it—and it was the misfortune of the erring pitcher to be in his way.

Tesrau, who knew all about Ty's bunt tactics, however, wasn't easily scared. He was a Giant, a John McGraw Giant.

"You try any business with me and I'll tear you apart," he shot back at the furious Cobb.

That particular meeting didn't take place. The pot boiled over before Ty got up to bat again.

Buck Herzog, another rip-'em-up, tear-'em-up Giant continued the ragging from his position at second base.

"Why don't you try to steal, Mr. Cobb? Second base is open, Mr. Cobb."

Ty didn't answer. His wrath was still pinned on Big Jeff.

"What's the matter, Mr. Cobb? Legs ain't what they used to be?"

Ty had enough.

On the pitch to the plate he reared off for the middle sack. Like a hare he went—but the Giants knew what was coming.

The pitch to the plate was wide, a pitchout, and the throw to second had Cobb by a mile.

That didn't deter the infuriated Georgian. Spikes way up, he went sliding into the bag.

The result was exactly what might have been expected. They grappled, rolled in the dirt, punched and banged at each other for all they were worth. When they were finally separated and thrown out of the field by the umpires, the ripped cloth showed where the Georgian's spikes had hit the Giant second baseman.

But that didn't end the chapter.

Both teams were staying at the same hotel. They met in the lobby. There were more words and Cobb kept his control as McGraw the Little Napoleon heaped insults on the Peach. For Herzog, however, the Georgian had nothing but contempt.

"Here's my room number," he said, "if you haven't had enough."

"I'll be there at ten o'clock," came back the game Buck.

And he was there, exactly at the appointed hour, with another buster-upper—Heinie Zimmerman.

It was a Pier six brawl but Herzog was no match for the six-foot one-hundred-and-eighty-pound, all-muscles Ty Cobb. The Georgian gave him a terrific shellacking but the Giant didn't let up until he was actually helpless.

It was a brutal fight and Ty Cobb took about as much as he could from the New York team. As a matter of fact, the Peach never played against the Giants again. He refused to play on the same field with them, packed his bag and did his training with the Cincinnati Reds and Christy Mathewson who was managing them. That, too, was something new in baseball, a player training with another club. It didn't seem to affect the Peach very much because, despite the so-so season of the Bengals, the Georgian regained his batting crown, his tenth, with a beautiful average of .383. Again he led his league with two hundred and twenty-five hits, in doubles with forty-four and in triples with twenty-three. He also maintained his pace in the stolen base department, leading the league for the third straight year, this time with fifty-five clean thefts to his credit.

The Giants, under McGraw, incidentally, won the National League flag in that tumultuous year, but the Georgian just kept rolling on his own pastures, building up one of the greatest names baseball would ever produce.

IN 1917 the United States was drawn into World War I. The sinking of the *Lusitania* with its fearful loss of American lives, the arrogant declaration of unrestricted submarine warfare by Kaiser Wilhelm of imperial Germany, the threat to the freedom of the seas, among other factors, sent America's doughboys into battle against the German Hun.

Everybody remembers that Hank Gowdy was the first baseball player to enlist. There were many others who joined up at once. But World War I, unlike World War II, was not an all-out, total conflict. Just a fraction of the more than eleven million men and women in service for the battle against the Nazis, the Japanese and Mussolini's Fascists were called into the armed forces in 1917. Nevertheless, any war must of necessity affect the American sport scene and in 1918 the roster of major league ballplayers in Uncle Sam's service was pretty large.

Ty Cobb enlisted. He had just completed another brilliant season on the diamond. Detroit had floundered to seventh place in the league standings but the Georgian had continued his almost unbelievable record at the bat. Again, and for the eleventh time in his career, he led the American loop in banging out those smart safeties. This time his average was .382. In ten straight seasons he had not once hit under .368, an amazing record, but it was still not the complete story of his astounding bat. In 1918 he put it all aside, however—his prodigious bat, his well-worn glove, his honed steel spikes—to join the forces fighting for America.

He got into the Chemical Warfare Division. In World War I the Germans used poison gas. Chemical warfare was in its infancy but its potential was great and awesome. The Peach got into the Chemical Division and, as might have been expected of the Georgian who always had to be first, he was quickly made a captain.

Shortly after Labor Day of 1918 Kaiser Wilhelm fled to Holland and the German war machine collapsed. November 11, 1918 was the date of the Armistice, and the world went wild with jubilation.

In 1919, the world, and especially America, wanted fun, wanted to have a good time, wanted to forget the horror of war. Baseball went into a boom year, the greatest year that baseball had ever experienced. The parks everywhere were jammed with fans and no park was big enough to house all the people who pushed their way into the stands, the grandstands and the bleachers alike. The front office rubbed its eyes and pinched itself to make sure it was awake, then counted the receipts to double check. It was true all right and there was only one thing to do: build bigger parks for more and better baseball.

Detroit shook itself out of its doldrums and climbed up to fourth place, while Ty Cobb, taking his old place in the field and his old turn at bat, banged out an average of .384 to retain his American League batting crown. This was his twelfth. It was also—and this is hard to say—his last.

No, Ty Cobb wasn't played out, not by a long shot. For years to come, for as many years as spans the lifetime baseball playing of some of the top-notch men in the game, the tireless Georgian would continue to bat them out at a terrific clip— over the .300 mark, over the .350 mark, yes, even over the .400 mark. In 1919 the Peach was only thirty-three years old, but thirty-three-year-olds on the diamond are generally already past their prime. Stan (The Man) Musial batted under .300 in his last few years as a player in his middle thirties. Joe DiMaggio at thirty-six retired from baseball at the close of the 1951 season. Ty Cobb was the batting champion of his league at the age of thirty-three. When he was almost thirty-six he played in ninety-nine games and whacked the ball, at the tremendous clip of .401. When he was forty-one years old he played in one hundred and four games and banged out the unbelievable average of .357 and was counted in the official averages among the five leading batters of the American League in that year. What's more, at that venerable age in any sport, with the possible exception of dominoes, checkers and the marathon, at the age of forty-one the irrepressible Georgian stole twenty-two bases, only five less than the league-leading George Sisler who stole twenty-seven that season.

The year 1919 was the last in which the Peach took the batting crown, the twelfth in his career, establishing just one of the countless records he put into the book, records which have yet to be equaled, but he was a long way from being through. At the drop of a hat he would take up any challenge that involved hitting or running. If a sports writer expressed the least sign of doubt, he would come out snarling to prove he was still top man.

They were tooting about the home run blasting of the Babe, and the tooting was all warranted. That didn't matter to the Peach. He went out there and hammered out five home runs in two consecutive games just to show them. Some newspaperman saw a youngster beat the Georgian in a foot race and wrote one of those solemn columns.

"The Georgia Peach is fading. He ain't what he used to be."

Cobb got madder than a hornet and called the newspaperman down to the field.

"Here," he said, pointing to a pair of specially weighted shoes. "This is what I was wearing yesterday. Feel them."

They were heavy all right, heavy with lead.

"Now go out there and watch me!" ordered the irate Cobb.

The reporter went out there and watched him. He saw the great Cobb flash around the base paths just as he did in the years gone by.

"I'm coming down!" he shouted.

And down he went, raising the dust, tearing up the turf, his steel spikes gleaming in the sun—under the tag of the eager second baseman for another stolen base.

THE Detroit Tigers hit the skids in 1920. This was the year Tris Speaker, playing his old outfield post for the Indians, managed them into their first pennant in the American League and led them to their first World's Championship to boot. This was also the year that Babe Ruth put on a Yankee uniform, banged out fifty-four home runs, woke up the fans to a new hero in baseball and filled the baseball parks—as no other player had done before—to witness the Sultan of Swat in action.

Ty Cobb watched the progress of these two rival outfielders, read and heard the acclaim the press and the public showered on them and, for the first time, wondered whether he had passed the peak of his career.

The complete failure of the Bengals who ended up seventh for their season's labors didn't help. Nor did the injuries which put the Peach on the side lines for more than forty games do anything for his morale. For once, in fourteen years, Ty Cobb was not even in the running for the batting crown of the league. He was not even counted among the first five. For twelve years out of his fifteen full seasons with the Tigers he had been top batsman in the junior circuit; once he had been second. In 1920, with a still very respectable average of .324, he was tenth in the order of leading hitters in the league.

But Ty Cobb wasn't one to brood. He set out at the end of the season for his usual fishing and hunting jaunt without the troubled mind which can haunt a player into the swift end of a career. He wanted to relax. He wanted to recuperate completely from the injuries he had suffered. He wanted to come back in 1921 with all the energy he knew he still possessed.

"There's plenty of baseball left in me," said the Peach. "I'm not through, not by a long shot."

And he certainly was not. There were still many years ahead for him, years that would prove to be as exciting, as thrilling, as swashbuckling as all the other years which had already made history for the Tigers, the American League and the name of the Georgia Peach. However, they were also going to be seasons of regret, disillusionment and disappointment. The trials of a manager of a big-league ball club are many and difficult. There is the pitcher the team needs and the manager knows where to get him, but the front office won't help. There's the infielder the office trades away, the infielder who spells the difference between victory and defeat. There are all the games lost by one run, games which might have been won by the pinch hitter the manager can't find. Then there are the hitters who go into a slump or the pitcher who suddenly goes sour. The life of the manager is one of constant turmoil, tension, even anguish and ulcers. Victories are sweet but victories are expected. It is the defeat which eats at the vital organs of the man who has to produce—not with his own bat and glove but with the skill of others. This is the lot that fell to Ty Cobb.

Ty didn't have to take on the seventh-place club. As a matter of fact, he hesitated when the front office offered him the job.

"I don't know whether I want that responsibility," he said. "I don't know whether playing regularly—as well as managing the team—is the best sort of arrangement."

And the Peach, who knew himself pretty well, modestly added, "I'm not sure I'd be a good manager. I don't know whether my abilities run in that direction."

But the front office, which had passed through one emotional crisis in letting Hughie Jennings go, despite all sentimental pressure, wasn't going to lose its argument with the Peach.

"Tris Speaker did it," they said. "You can do it, too."

Ty pondered that one. The Gray Eagle had been the one man to challenge his leadership in the league. Together with Babe Ruth, it would be Speaker and Cobb for the all-time, all-great outfield.

"It's worth a try, I suppose," he said, and he remembered again, as he often remembered, his father's "Don't come home a failure." And he remembered the first time he had said, "I'm first. I'm always first."

"I'll take it," he said, and in the spring of 1921 he took over and began to whip the Detroit Tigers, who had assembled in San Antonio, Texas, into what he hoped would be a club to challenge Tris Speaker's Cleveland Indians.

The Peach had been in the habit of reporting late for spring training and it never had seemed to have any effect on hitting or fielding. But he was the manager now, and he was down in Texas with the first blade of grass in the fields. He was a fighting manager and a talking manager. No one in the game knew baseball better than Tyrus—and from early morning till curfew he bustled among his players, showing a man how to improve his stance at the plate, how to improve his cut at the ball, how to take that extra base on a clout to the outfield, how to steal that base when they needed it. And when they weren't on the field, when they were eating or just sitting around gabbing, it was more baseball, the finer points—and Cobb knew them all.

There was nothing but baseball at the spring headquarters of the Detroit Bengals. And once the regulation season got under way, the team showed that it had put its training to good use. From seventh place in the order of batting averages, the Tigers leaped to the Number One spot. Harry Heilmann, whom Manager Cobb had shifted from first to the outfield, banged out the ball to the tune of .394 and the league's crown in that department. At first base Ty put Lu Blue, who had the hearts of Detroit for a long, long time. The new Tiger manager also developed a couple of hard-hitting catchers for his squad—Larry Woodall who hit .363 and Johnny Bassler who hit .306. The club's batting average zoomed to .316.

The team hit beautifully but the front office didn't do anything about getting a decent pitching corps for their new manager. The Tigers scored eight hundred and eighty-three runs but their opposition scored eight hundred and fifty-two, and that was better than five plus per game, too. Ty had the club in the first divison for a good part of his first managerial year, but since no team can get anywhere without two or three men who can pitch nine innings regularly, Detroit ended its year in sixth place.

As for the Peach's personal record, there can be no question about the wear and tear his new responsibilities placed on him. Still he whacked out one hundred and ninety-seven hits for an average of .389, just five points under the league-leading Bengal, Heilmann, and stole twenty-two bases. One can only speculate on what the great Cobb might have done had he not been burdened with the aches and pains of piloting a club which was going nowhere in particular. Certainly he should have experienced very little difficulty in regaining once more the slugging leadership of his circuit.

However, if Ty gave it any thought at all he didn't let anyone know about it.

"Watch us next year," he said, and began to knock at the door of the front office for a couple of much-needed infielders and especially for a little pitching assistance.

And Frankie Navin of the front office came through nicely. He got Elmo Rigney for shortstop and George Cutshaw for second. They were a couple of good boys and their presence showed up in the won and lost columns. He also brought to the club one of the fattest men who have ever played big league ball, Robert Roy Fothergill. He tipped the scale at more than two hundred pounds and was as round as a ball. Everybody called him Fat Fothergill but no man enjoyed the good will and the good wishes of the fans more than this slugging outfielder. He was fat, he was popular, and he was amazingly easy on his feet, considering the man's bulk. More than once he tickled the fancy of his admirers by doing a complete somersault without touching the ground with his finger.

But more important than the infielders and Bob Fothergill, Navin brought two pitchers to Detroit, two of the best boys from the Pacific Coast League —Herman Pillette and Sylvester Johnson. Pillette won nineteen games for the club that year, and with Bobbie Veach needled into hitting .327, Fothergill .322, Heilmann .356 and Ty Cobb .401, the Detroit Tigers catapulted themselves into third place for the year.

Of course Detroit was jubilant and the front office quite pleased with the lift the Georgia Peach had given the club. But most amazing was the terrific clouting of the irrepressible Georgian. Only once before in the majors had a man hit over .400 three times in his career. Jesse Burkett had done it, playing for Cleveland and the St. Louis Cardinals. Now there were two of them, Burkett and Cobb. In all baseball history the feat has never been matched except by one other ballplayer, the magnificent Rogers Hornsby. The longer Cobb played the greater his record grew, and in 1922 there seemed to be no horizon to the possibilities of the clouting Cobb.

In 1923 the Tigers, with Ty at the helm, kept moving. And if the front office hadn't pulled a boner—trading away the young pitcher Howard Ehmke, who won twenty games for the last-place Red Sox—Cobb might have attained that prize which he was never to get, first place in the American League. As it was, with the team continuing to be one of the greatest hitting squads in the story of baseball, the Detroit Tigers came in that year second only to the New York Yankees and their home-run-belting George Herman Ruth.

The Tigers were moving and everybody, including the Peach, was pleased with the progress they were making.

"The Team that wins the pennant," said Tyrus, at the beginning of the 1924 season, "will have to beat Detroit."

It was a pretty good prophecy. The Tigers were in first place, or just under it, all April, May, June and July. In August there were three days when the Bengals led the league. And throughout the season the Ty Cobb charges trimmed the three-time pennant-winning Yankees, taking the season's series thirteen to nine. But if this wasn't a Yankee year, neither was it the year for Cobb.

The Peach had Charlie Gehringer playing second base for part of the season but he wasn't quite ripe for his great major league career. He also acquired Earl Whitehill, who won seventeen games for Detroit that year, and who would continue to be a regular winner for the auto town for a long time. But they weren't enough to offset the terrific surge of the boys from Washington who, led by the mighty Bucky Harris, brought the capital city its first American League banner.

Detroit, for all of its turbulent victories over the Yankees—and they were very turbulent—came in third, behind the much-hated New Yorkers.

Whenever the Yankees came to Detroit, or the Tigers to Yankee Stadium, there was tension and hatred that might explode at a moment's notice. There was one grand melee which resulted in a forfeited game and a nine to nothing victory for the Yanks.

Bob Meusel didn't like the ball Bert Cole tossed up to the plate. It hit him in the back and Bob, generally one of the quieter men on the field, hurled his bat at the pitcher, then rushed out to the mound. And before anyone could stop them, both Meusel and Cole were throwing punches at each other.

That was the spark that set the whole feud really going. Yankees and Tigers, every one of them, were at one another's throats. Cobb came down on a tear from the outfield and piled into the innocent Babe Ruth.

Nor was that all. The spectators joined in the fun. It was a sight rarely, if ever, witnessed in baseball before and the boys had to pay for it. Ban Johnson immediately suspended the otherwise peaceful Bob Meusel and pitcher Cole at once, called for a flock of reports from everybody involved and ended up by slapping ten-day leaves-without-pay for the two men who had started the ruckus—fining Meusel one hundred dollars, Cole and Babe Ruth fifty dollars. Ty got away scot free and so did everyone else, for some unexplained reason.

It was a rough-and-tumble year for the Detroit Tigers. Every year, with Ty Cobb at the helm, was rough and tumble. But after coming up with the near champions in 1924, just five games short of the pennant, the Bengals began to fall apart, slowly at first, but then with alarming rapidity.

They always could hit. With the Peach showing them how it was done, they couldn't miss. Harry Heilmann kept coming in with the batting title every other year, Red Wingo kept hitting the ball well over the .350 mark. Heinie Manush was the league's top batter in 1926, while Ty, himself, kept busting the apple all over the lot. In 1923 his average was .340, in 1924 it was .338, in 1925 he climbed again to .378 and in 1926 it was .339. But

Earl Whitehill flopped in his second year out with the Tigers. The rest of the pitching corps didn't measure up for a team that could contend for the league leadership, and the perpetual infield troubles, which plagued the Georgian throughout his tenure as manager of the club, were not helped by the beaning of the promising young shortstop Rigney.

In 1925 the feeble Tiger dropped to fourth place; in 1926 it fell to sixth.

Cobb didn't feel good about it. He was bitterly disappointed. Failure rankled in him. It was something he could never accept. He could get his boys to hit but he couldn't make star pitchers out of bush-leaguers, classy infielders out of men who weren't good enough to make the big-time grade.

"Won't the folks back home be proud of you when they read you're winning one game after another with your clouting?" he would say to a Bengal, pulling him aside before game time.

And the boy would go out there and slam the ball for all he was worth.

"We need this game," he would confide to one of his pitchers. "You can do it. I know you can do it—and I'm counting on you."

And occasionally the hurler would respond and pitch a brilliant nine innings, pitch way over his head for Cobb to win that game.

He got Harry Heilmann to call Veach every name in the book—and some that aren't—to get the outfielder sore enough to take it out on the ball. Veach would never speak to Heilmann for Harry's good efforts but he did become one of Detroit's great batsmen.

Ty knew how to get at his men. But cajoling, praise, pleas and pressure aren't enough to win on the diamond. You need skill, plenty of skill, and it was the skill which was missing in the Detroit roster.

After the game, lost by an error, lost by the failure of the shortstop to close in a gap, lost by the sad hurling of his pitchers, Ty would leave the clubhouse quietly, get into his car and, as fast as he could, drive to his home on the outskirts of Detroit.

Here was his family—his wife, his children—Tyrus, Shirley, Herschel, Beverly, Howell—and here he loosened up. Howell tugged at his trouser leg, Beverly climbed onto his lap.

Shirley and Tyrus, Jr. prepared the evening meals every now and then, and that was the way Cobb wanted it.

"I like them to share in the family responsibilities," he said.

They couldn't do as well down in Georgia in a house full of servants.

"I want them to get an understanding of the value of money," he said.

The Peach knew very well what money meant. He had already amassed a tidy fortune, on his own.

"I want them to know how people live, and think and work," he said. "I want them to grow up democratic Americans."

At home he was a new man. All the heartaches

182

of the diamond were shoved into some small corner of his mind.

"My home," he said, "and my wife and my family come first with me."

But in 1926 the Tigers dropped to seventh place in the American League and Ty Cobb handed Frank Navin his resignation as manager of the Detroit Bengals, and his Tiger uniform as well.

For 22 years he had played for Detroit. He had played in 2,804 games for the Tigers, been at bat 10,586 times, hammered out 3,902 hits, scored 2,176 runs and stolen 865 bases. His twenty-two-year batting average with the team was .3689. Truly he had given Detroit what no other man had ever given to a baseball club. Here were scores of records which would stand unmatched for years to come. Here were scores of records which have yet to be approached. He came to Detroit an eighteen-year-old boy. He left them a forty-year-old man who could still bat well over .300 and steal his quota of bases to boot. He should have left Detroit in a blaze of glory. But the seventh-place team had shadowed the brilliant record of the Georgian.

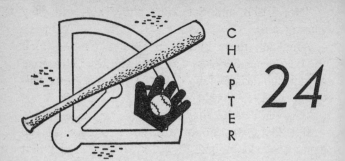

BEFORE the fans had quite recovered from the shock of the announcement that Ty Cobb would no longer manage the Detroit Tigers, would no longer play in a Bengal uniform, baseball fandom was handed another and even more surprising jolt with the news that Tris Speaker had resigned from the Cleveland Indians. Not everyone in the auto town had been happy with Cobb runnings its club. There had been plenty of yelping for his managerial scalp. But no one had even thought of asking for the head of the Gray Eagle. The fans sensed that there was something not quite right —two great stars of the game leaving the diamond within a few weeks of each other. There was talk and some of that talk didn't sound too good.

"Men like Cobb and Speaker don't quit overnight," they said.

"They're being railroaded out," they said.

"It can't be that they're mixed up in something crooked?" they asked, hesitatingly.

184

"Not Cobb and Speaker," they said, but they weren't sure.

After all, there had been Eddie Cicotte, Buck Weaver, even Shoeless Joe Jackson who had gone wrong and let the fans down in the notorious sellout of the 1919 World Series.

"Not the Peach," they said. "Not the Eagle."

But there was doubt and for the good of the game that doubt had to be cleared up. And that was exactly what the venerable, white-headed commissioner of baseball Judge Kenesaw Mountain Landis did. In late December of 1926 he opened the books, sifted truth from rumor and let everyone in on the affairs which had been hushed up, the affairs which had led to the resignation of two of the greatest names in baseball.

Dutch Leonard (not to be confused with the knuckleballer who pitched in later years), who had pitched for Detroit and who had been released to the minors by the Georgia Peach, had started the fireworks going, and the noise they made came close to destroying the nation's confidence and support of its national pastime, came close to destroying baseball itself.

According to the newspaper reports of December 26, 1926, Leonard asserted that he, Cobb, Speaker and Wood, who was then pitching for Cleveland, met under the grandstand at Navin Field, Detroit, on September 24, 1919, and agreed that Detroit would be allowed to win its game with Cleveland on the following day, thus clenching third place in the American League pennant race.

Still, there was enough here for an investigation, enough here to blow the ground from under two of the greatest stars in the story of the diamond, enough to blow that diamond all apart.

Ban Johnson, tempestuous president of the American League, acted fast. He always acted fast.

He called the two men, produced the letters Leonard had put into evidence and asked both Cobb and Speaker to quit their teams, to quit the game.

"For the good of the game," he said, "to save the game," he emphasized, "I think it would be best if both you and Speaker resigned. We don't need the scandal and neither do you."

"I'm innocent of all these charges," declared Cobb, hotly. "I never quit under fire. I'm not quitting now."

"And I'm right with Cobb," said Speaker, more quietly. "You've just got a pack of lies in those letters. I'm sticking to my job and I'm sticking to baseball."

Ban Johnson was never a man who was easily moved from a position, once he had taken that position.

"I haven't passed judgment on you," he declared. "I'm thinking of how this stuff will sound in the papers. I'm thinking of what the fans will say. I'm thinking of what this smear will do to your names and to your families. Do you want all this muck spilled all over you and your wives and your kids in every paper in the country?"

"My wife and my family come first," Ty Cobb

186

had said, and he meant it. It wasn't easy to take Ban Johnson's orders, it wasn't easy to retreat before an attack, a vile attack, but there were his wife and his kids.

"I'll resign," he said, so quietly Ban Johnson could hardly hear him.

And Speaker, the Gray Eagle, lowered his head and accepted the terms of the hardfisted president of the league.

But the smoke of rumors had to lift and when Judge Landis decided to bring the whole story before the public, declaring that rumor, idle rumor, is always more dangerous than truth, the two all-time greats came to one and the same conclusion.

"We can't take this lying down," they said. "The thing's a lie and the lie will do more damage to baseball than the facts. We will stick to the facts and the facts will show us innocent of any attempt to corrupt the game. We don't want to leave the game with any stain of mud on us. Our good names and the names of our families will rest on the fight we will make against these charges. And we will fight!"

Judge Landis asked Dutch Leonard to present his evidence in Chicago, where he had arranged for a meeting with everybody involved. But Leonard did not make the trip to Chicago.

The judge traveled to California, and there he collected the Leonard statement.

Smokey Joe came down from Yale where he was coaching. Cobb and Speaker both showed up at the commissioner's office.

"I have been in baseball twenty-two years," declared Cobb for the press, on his way to the meeting, and there were tears in his eyes as he spoke. "I have played the game as hard and square and clean as any man ever did. All I thought of was to win. My conscience is clear. I will rest my case with the American fans and will match my record in baseball against that of anybody connected with the game."

To the commissioner, Cobb declared, "I have never been involved in fixing a game. I have never bet on an American League game, never!"

Speaker was less vehement than the Peach but no less firm.

"Ever since I became manager of the Cleveland Club I did everything I could, legally, to win every game we played."

The *New York Journal American* quoted Smokey Joe as saying:

"Leonard had seven years to frame a story around those two letters and he was very bitter against Cobb because Cobb had released him. I guess he was also bitter against Speaker because Speaker didn't claim him on waivers and keep him in the league. He wanted to get those two fellows and he didn't care who he got, as long as he reached his end. That is the way it looks to me."

Fans from coast to coast were shocked by the revelations. They didn't know what to think. Here were two of the greatest men in the history of the game, two men who had been followed, emulated, worshiped for years by millions of boys

188

and grown men—and here they were, their great names sullied and dirtied and dragged into the mud.

"If Leonard had anything on me," Cobb said, "do you think I would have released him from the club in 1925?"

"Look at the box score of that game they said I threw," said Speaker. "I got up five times and banged out three hits. Two of them were triples. Does that look like I was dumping?" The fans roused themselves. Thousands of letters poured into the homes of the accused men, supporting them, declaring their faith in them. Thousands of letters hit the front offices of the Tigers and the Indians, demanding the reinstatement of the stars. Sportswriters all over the country came to their defense.

"We want to express to you and Tris Speaker our utmost confidence in your honesty and integrity," came one letter from the Philadelphia Sports Writers Association.

"The sporadic outbursts have in no way lowered you from the pedestal as the greatest ballplayer of all time," came another to the entrenched Georgia Peach.

"We deem it a privilege to invite you as a guest of honor to our annual banquet."

The Augusta Chamber of Commerce arranged a testimonial dinner for its favorite son.

Clark Griffith spoke up from Washington.

"I have known Cobb and Speaker ever since they have been in the game and I am satisfied as to their honesty."

189

Offers of money to aid in their defense came rushing through the mails from every part of the country, but Cobb and Speaker were ready to put their fortunes on the line to save their honor. And they did.

According to *The New York Times* of January 2, 1927, Risberg had told Landis that the Tigers and the White Sox had fixed their four-game series on the Labor Day week end of 1917.

Twenty-nine players demanded that they be heard by the commissioner and twenty-nine angry men confronted Risberg in the judge's office. Ty Cobb was there and Eddie Collins, Ray Schalk, Harry Heilmann, Howard Ehmke, Bob Veach and George Harper—and the white-haired judge had to step in between Donie Bush and Swede Risberg to prevent the former star shortstop from punching his accuser in the nose.

Not one voice supported the man who had been kicked out of professional baseball. Even Buck Weaver, who had gone the way of the Black Sox in company with Risberg, spoke out against his former teammate—and the commissioner's decision was a foregone conclusion.

"There is no evidence," declared Kenesaw Landis, "that the Tiger-White Sox games in 1917 were in any way tampered with. The charges against the men accused have no foundation whatever in fact. They are all innocent."

The fans breathed a very audible sigh of relief. That was one threat removed. But there was still the other threat. The Speaker-Cobb decision was still to be made. There could be no peace, no sense of assurance among the fans until Landis would speak again, make the fateful decision on the Gray Eagle and the Georgia Peach.

The judge was a careful man, a hard man, but just. He took his time, weighed the evidence carefully. He wanted to make no mistake. He would make his decision only after he had weighed all the words spoken, all the written words, after he had examined every shred involved in the accusation and in the defense.

But the judge was also a man of great consideration. He didn't keep the American fans waiting any longer than was necessary.

Very shortly after the decision on the Risberg affair, he handed down his verdict on the Peach and the Eagle.

"Ty Cobb and Tris Speaker," he declared crisply, "have not been—nor are they now—guilty of ever fixing the outcome of a baseball game. They are Not Guilty! Their names are restored to the reserve lists of their clubs!"

Never did the boys and the men—and the women, too—who watch the game or play the game, on sandlot or on glistening diamond, join in such single-minded rejoicing. Cobb and Speaker were back with them. Their great names showed bolder and greater for the ordeal they had suffered.

"You'll never see their likes again!"

"Great men!"

"Both of them!"

"You'll never see greater!"

And Tris Speaker said, quietly, "I'll be in a uniform, a baseball uniform, with the opening of the season."

Ty Cobb was less sure.

"I don't know," he said. "I'm not sure."

CHAPTER 25

COBB was a free agent in 1927 and there was a mad scramble in both leagues to land the Peach. He was a prize for any major league club and the bidding for his services was high and frantic. It took Connie Mack and about seventy thousand dollars to get the Georgian to wear the uniform of the Philadelphia Athletics. The Mackmen, more than any other club in the league, had hated the Peach. The words that had passed between Ty and Connie's boys were hot enough to burn up the ball park. The police had had to be called out to protect the Georgian from the wrath of the Philadelphia fans. But when Cobb came out into Shibe Park in the uniform of the City of Brotherly Love all was forgotten, the feuding and the fighting, the spiking of Frank (Home run) Baker and everything else. Ty Cobb, the Georgia Jewel, was one of the boys, one of Connie Mack's boys, and all Philadelphia swelled its chest with pride. The greatest man in the history of baseball was theirs.

Ty found himself in the midst of a lot of great old-timers that year. There was the all-time-great Eddie Collins, Zack Wheat who had worn the heart of Brooklyn on his sleeve for almost twenty years. Tris Speaker would have been there but Clark Griffith had come first and the Gray Eagle was playing for the Washington Senators. There were other familiar faces, however, with Philadelphia that year. There was his old pitcher Howard Ehmke and the younger stars, Bishop and Al Simmons. It was quite a team Connie had assembled, a fighting, hustling team, and Cobb was right at home with them.

The Peach was forty years old, and most ballplayers retire long before that hoary age for an athlete, but the Georgian was in there, punching and belting the old apple as if he were hardly out of his rookie years, stealing those bases as if he hadn't yet reached his voting age. Nor had he lost any of his lust for winning, nor any of his readiness to bring his jaw and even his fists, when necessary, into action.

It started even before the Mackmen got up to their home park. They were playing an exhibition game with the Boston Braves at St. Petersburg in Florida and Cobb was giving Umpire Wilson some words of advice, some words of criticism and a little of his private opinion of the arbiter's eyesight and general ability.

Suddenly the umpire, who evidently couldn't take it too well, snapped off his mask, turned to Cobb on the bench and ordered him out of the park.

"Get out, Cobb!" he yelled, red in the face. "Get out of the park!"

Ty was an old hand at this sort of diplomacy. Quick as a flash he was on his feet, moving toward the plate and the umpire. And Wilson, his mask swinging menacingly in his hand, came forward to meet him.

"Go ahead and start something!" shouted the tempestuous Georgian. "Start something and I'll show you!"

"Get out," repeated the frustrated Wilson.

But Ty took his time, strolled over to the bench, took a long drink of water, fussed around with his glove, picked up a bottle of pop, sat down on the bench and calmly began to drink it.

Wilson, completely beside himself, turned to the crowd.

"This game is forfeited," he declared, and as the crowd sat in stunned silence he walked off the field.

Wilson seemed to have the habit of throwing men out of the game. One afternoon he had thrown eleven Yankees out of the ball park—another afternoon a batch of Boston ballplayers and two policemen along with them.

Connie Mack was furious with the arbiter's action.

"The people were out there to see Cobb play and one man with a little petty authority spoiled their afternoon."

But the commissioner slapped a hundred-dollar fine on the Peach for his performance.

Right at the beginning of his first season with Connie, Ty got into one of the more tempestuous affairs which spiced his career.

Philadelphia was playing the Red Sox. It was a close game. The score was three to two in favor of Boston over the Mackmen when Cobb came up to bat in the last of the eighth inning.

Hooks Wiltse tossed the Peach one he liked and he sent it booming over the right field fence just like that, and the Philadelphia fans let out a lusty cheer for the new Mackman.

But Red Ormsby called the Peach back to the plate.

"Strike," he said. "It was a foul. Strike!"

The whole Philadelphia squad was at his throat.

"What do you mean, foul?"

"That was a home run!"

"It cleared the fence!"

"Yes," said the redheaded umpire, as calmly as he could. "It cleared the fence and it was fair when it cleared the fence."

"Then it's a homer!" shouted the Mackmen.

"It turned foul after it cleared the fence," said the unwavering arbiter, and no argument could move him.

Ty picked up his bat, tapped the plate. Wiltse wound up and sent the ball down. The Peach pulled his bat back to take his swat at the ball, and the bat poked Umpire Red Ormsby sharply in his chest.

"Get out!" ordered the irate umpire.

Ty had heard that remark before.

"You don't think I'm going to let you get away with it, do you?" stormed the redhead. "Get out!"

"Accident!" said Ty.

"Accident, my foot!" exclaimed the umpire. "Out!"

And Ty was out but that wasn't the end of it.

Simmons was next up and he had a few words to offer Red Ormsby, and Ormsby had a few of his own for Simmons.

The fans caught on and began to shout their own opinions down on the field.

Simmons shoved Ormsby back on his heels—pushed him.

"Out!" ordered the umpire. "Get out of the park!"

The fans began to throw bottles, and it took a little while before the game could get on.

Immediately, as might have been expected, Ty and Simmons had fines slapped on them, and "indefinite suspension."

This was bad enough for ordinary times. It was especially bad because the Athletic were scheduled to open in Detroit and Detroit's fans, who had not forgotten the old Peach, were preparing a gigantic welcome for him.

Protests poured into Ban Johnson's office, but a protest would never move the stanch president of the American League. Pleas were sent in to him, and the pleas probably worked. Whichever it was, the suspension of Cobb was lifted only a few hours before game time, and Detroit was jubilant.

There was a testimonial luncheon at the Masonic

Temple, a parade to Navin Field, led by a police motorcycle escort and a military band. At the park they presented the man who had given Detroit so much of his life with an automobile and a host of other gifts. And in the evening there was another dinner in honor of the great star.

"We're here to let Ty Cobb know," said the toastmaster at the luncheon, "that we're with him, win, lose or draw. Although he was born in Georgia, his real home is in the hearts of the Detroit fans."

Mayor John Smith was there, and also his old teammate George Moriarty who was now managing the Tigers, and Connie Mack and Fielding Yost and Benny Friedman of football fame. And they all were in the park when Ty got up to bat, the fans roaring their greetings. And the great Cobb answered their greeting as best he could—with his bat. Whitehill pitched it and the Georgian whacked it, a clean two-bagger and the fans again shook the stadium with their great shout of approval.

"I am grateful to all of you," said Cobb, his voice husky with emotion. "You are very kind. It affects me deeply."

If only his father were there to see, old Herschel Cobb who had said to his son, "Don't come home a failure!"

The Peach had come home. And the halls rang with the glorious fame he had brought to the name of the boy from Royston, Tyrus Raymond Cobb.

For two years the Georgian played for Connie

Mack, and he gave the great manager all he had, and that was plenty.

"Cobb Hits Homer, Athletics Win," ran the sports headline.

"Cobb Bangs in Winning Run."

"The Peach Steals Home."

"Cobb . . . Cobb . . . Cobb. . . ."

In 1927 the Peach played in one hundred and thirty-four games for Connie Mack, banged out one hundred and seventy-five hits, thirty-two of them doubles, seven of them triples, five of them homers, all for a brilliant average of .357. He scored one hundred and four runs in the process and stole twenty-two bases, just five under the mark made by Sisler who led the league with twenty-seven. Pretty good for a man approaching his forty-first birthday.

In 1928 the Georgian slowed down a bit. He hit for only .323. What a mark for a man who had been playing the big time for twenty-four years! What a mark for any big-leaguer to shoot for!

Maybe there was more baseball left in the Peach, good baseball, even great baseball, but no one was ever to find out.

"I'd rather retire," said Ty, "while I've still a bit of the taste of glory."

And he folded his suit neatly and packed it away. And he laid his bats down on his suit. And he laid his glove on his bats. And never again, would the great Georgia Peach carry his sticks to the plate in a regulation game, never again would his spikes go flashing in the sun, never again would the dust

199

swirl up around second, hiding the bag, hiding the ball, hiding the greatest player of them all.

This was the end of the greatest career in baseball. This was the end of his playing days. It was not, however, the end of the songs in praise of the great Peach.

THERE have been great names in baseball, names of men who will live as heroes as long as kids choose up sides and lay out a diamond on some empty lot. Rube Waddell, Nap Lajoie, Hans Wagner, the Big Train, Big Six, the Babe, Stan the Man, Ted Williams, Willie Mays—each a great figure in a pastime which year in and year out grips the hearts and the spirits of our entire nation. And each of these men, and countless others, have left behind them a rich heritage for the years they gave to the baseball parks from coast to coast and from the Great Lakes to the Gulf of Mexico. But no one left behind so rich a heritage as the Georgia Peach when he closed the chapter on his playing days at the end of that season in 1928.

There were ninety records he had established before he hung up his mitt, ninety records unmatched and unbeaten. No one could or, in all probability, ever will boast such a mark. It is almost unbelievable, and still the books are there to show

it. And most of those records the Peach established, the great majority of them have yet to be
beaten, or even reached.

He played 24 years in the major leagues and no
one had played—or has played since—so many
years in the big time.

He played in 3,033 games, a mark that can
scarcely be approached.

The Peach was at bat 11,429 times, and that's a
tremendous number of times. The young ballplayers coming up into the majors can only stare at that
record and wonder how it can be possible.

He collected 4,191 hits for his 24 years, an average of more than 174 hits per season over the long-
est span of major league hitting in the books.

He has more singles to his credit than any man
who has carried a bat to the plate—3,052.

He collected more three-baggers, 297, than any
other man in his playing lifetime.

He established the record for most extra base hits,
topping all the sluggers with 1,139.

He has the greatest number of total bases ever
collected—5,863.

No man has ever scored as many runs as did the
Peach—2,244.

No one has approached his lifetime batting average of .367.

He was batting champion for 12 seasons and that
is a record to shoot at.

In 23 seasons he hit over .300.

In 9 seasons he collected more than 200 hits.

For 13 times he banged out 5 hits in 5 times at bat.

Only two men are tied with him for hitting over .400 for 3 seasons.

But no one can begin to approach his stolen base total of 892.

These are only some of the marks the great Cobb established in his long and magnificent career on the diamond, marks to wonder at, marks to acclaim, marks which logically place the Georgian as the Number One man in baseball history.

And that was exactly how they saw it, when in 1936 a nation-wide poll conducted by the Baseball Writers Association placed Ty Cobb as the Number One man for the Cooperstown Baseball Hall of Fame.

There were 226 votes cast by the sports writers from all over the country and of the 226, 222 named the Georgia Peach. He fell 4 votes short of a perfect score, but there were some young reporters among those who sent in their ballots and perhaps all they knew of Cobb was by reputation. Eight years had elapsed since the Peach had turned in his spikes and eight years can be a long time.

Still 222 votes were more votes in the tabulation than were recorded for any other man nominated for the Cooperstown memorial to the game, 7 more votes than were cast for the greatest shortstop of all time, Hans Wagner, and 7 more votes than were sent in for the baseball hero of the hour, the belting Bambino of the Ruppert Rifles, George Herman Ruth.

Fourth man on the list was Big Six, the immortal Christy Mathewson with 205 ballots, 17 behind the perpetual leader Cobb. Fifth was the Big Train, the man whose fast ball is legend, Walter Johnson, with 189 votes.

And that, in 1936, closed the list of those who had been elected to grace baseball's brand-new Hall of Fame. The rules required that a Hall-of-Famer receive 75% of the vote cast. Ty Cobb had polled over 98%, Wagner and Ruth over 95%, Mathewson over 90% and Johnson 83%. The others, many whose names would join them later, fell by the wayside.

Nap Lajoie polled 146 votes, Tris Speaker 133, Cy Young 111, Rogers Hornsby, new manager of the St. Louis Browns, 105, the fiery Mickey Cochrane 80.

The list was long. George Sisler got 77 votes, Eddie Collins, another all-time great, got only 60, the great Grover Cleveland Alexander collected only 55 votes, Columbia Lou Gehrig 51. The Little Napoleon, John McGraw 4, Chief Bender 2, Connie Mack, Frank (Home run) Baker, Dazzy Vance, Dizzy Dean, Charlie Gehringer one apiece.

There were other names, many names. Baseball history is jam-packed with great performers, great stars. It is no easy task for a sports writer, especially for those who are best informed on the game, to choose from all these brilliant players and say this one or that one was or is the greatest of them all. There was no question about Ty Cobb, however. He stood head and shoulders above all the rest. No man had ever achieved so much in baseball. No man had given so much to the game.

There was another poll, back in 1942, and this poll was limited to big-league managers, men who had once been managers and to the great players of all time. They cast one vote each and that vote was for the man whom they considered to be the greatest star who ever played on the diamond.

There were 102 votes in all and 14 men were nominated for the signal honor. And of those 102, the Georgia Peach, Tyrus Raymond Cobb, collected 60 ballots, a clean majority. Of the remaining 42 votes, Hans Wagner came in second with 17 ballots, 43 full votes behind the Georgian. Babe Ruth copped 11 votes, 49 behind the Peach. The 14 remaining ballots were divided among the 11 remaining players honored. Roger Hornsby picked up 4 votes, the others one each. What a tribute to the man and the player—Ty Cobb! Certainly no one can judge better the merits of a ballplayer than those who play the game, and with no doubt at all they had chosen Cobb the greatest of all.

"Ty Cobb is undoubtedly the greatest player I ever saw on the diamond," said the venerable Connie Mack.

"The greatness of Ty Cobb was something to be seen," said George Sisler. "His hitting, his running, the way he played the outfield, to see him was to remember him forever."

The quotes can be matched a hundred times, and every quote from a star whose brilliance on the diamond will never be forgotten. Ty Cobb was a man who gave everything he had to the ball game, and the fans knew it and appreciated it. The ballplayers themselves, those who played with him and those who played against him, knew it, too. And everyone—fan, sports writer and ballplayer—bestowed on him the title he deserved, the Greatest Player in the History of Baseball.

Number One in baseball's Hall of Fame, the magnificent Ty Cobb's hat, his glove, his flashing spikes hang in the museum at Cooperstown, in tribute to the man, and an everlasting reminder of his singular greatness on the diamond.

AND what does a man do when he retires? What does a man do who has spent more than twenty-five years of hammering a ball out of the infield, speeding after flies in the outfield, running those base paths like a whirlwind?

The Georgia Peach always loved his fishing and there was plenty of time for casting and reeling now. He loved his hunting and there was more time than he needed for the gun and the trek through the woods. There was time for his dogs, too. The Georgian always had a soft spot for dogs, the ones with the long pedigrees and those the kids find wandering around the park somewhere, without a collar or a tag or a name.

The Peach gave a lot of thought to kids, and a lot of time. He participated actively in *Esquire's* All-American Boys Baseball games, organized by Joe Hendrickson, famous Minneapolis sportswriter, and, along with such baseball greats as Hans Wagner and Babe Ruth, managed a team for the championship clashes.

The Georgian also took a hand at golf and did better than fair on the links. In 1937 he won the California Indians' golf tournament. In 1941 he met his old rival, the Bambino Babe Ruth, and on the Fresh Meadow course in Long Island, in a match arranged for the benefit of charities, he took the Babe in camp, three and two.

There was a lot the Peach could do.

There were no financial worries. He had amassed a rather magnificent fortune, evaluated at one time at somewhere in the neighborhood of seven million dollars. He could do pretty well what he wanted— and he did.

In 1948 he put up one hundred thousand dollars to construct a modern hospital in his home town of Royston. He had wanted to be a doctor when he was just a little fellow. Baseball got him instead. Putting up a hospital was next best. The hospital was constructed in honor of his father and mother. The doctor who was to be put in charge of the medical building was Dr. Stewart Brown, the same Stewart Brown who, as a kid, had pitched them in to the Peach, the Stewart Brown who might have added another great name to the roster of greats in baseball but chose medicine instead.

"I'm glad to be able to do it," said Tyrus, and he was thinking of the little boy who had dreamed of the operating room, the white walls and the clinical stillness. "I'm glad to be able to do it for Royston." And he wondered, as he often wondered in those days, whether he had chosen wisely—the clashing drama of baseball and not the hushed drama of surgery. "I'm glad to be able to do it for Dr. Stewart Brown, and for all the good people of my home town."

"My only regret," concluded the Peach, "is that my father is not with us to witness the construction of this memorial to a man who gave so much of his life to the betterment of the state of Georgia."

Ty Cobb was a man of deep feeling. He was more the man of action. Out of the limelight of baseball he went into the limelight of business. He was a retired man but no retired man ever covered the mileage that Cobb covered. No man ever stayed less in one fixed spot. He was on the go all the time. Every day you picked up the papers you read—about Cobb in a different baseball training camp, in a different baseball park, talking to young players, talking to the stars, advising, suggesting, coaching, demonstrating.

His children had grown up by this time and were out on their own. He saw little of his wife, Charlotte, then less. They drifted apart. Inevitably, in 1947, they were divorced. At about this time, the Peach began to see a lot of his old friend Dr. John Fairbairn, a specialist in Buffalo, and more of the doctor's daughter Frances Cass. A romance blossomed and bloomed and in September, 1949, Ty married again and Frances Cass became the second Mrs. Tyrus Raymond Cobb.

This might have seemed to be the end of the story of the Peach, a retired millionaire with homes in

Nevada, California and Georgia, but it was not. Before he died Cobb continued to pop in and out of the limelight for years after he had apparently retired. For example, when Congress decided to investigate baseball's big headache, its reserve clause, the Number One man they called on was, of course, Ty Cobb. This was in July, 1951. And the Georgian, more than twenty years away from his last game in the majors, was sharp and precise in his judgment.

"Baseball is a sport," he said, crisply. "It's never been a business."

About the hot reserve clause, "It keeps the rich clubs from gobbling up all the good players," he said, "but a special appeal board for the players wouldn't do anybody any harm."

The congressmen asked the Georgian some questions about one of his salary disputes with Frank Navin and Ty pleaded a "faulty memory." But there was nothing wrong with his memory when they brought up the fifty dollars the National Baseball Commission had fined him during an argument with Navin, president of the Detroit Tigers.

"I never paid that fine," he said, with a wink of his eye. "Maybe Mr. Navin paid it but I never did."

He wasn't on the diamond, he wasn't hitting it where no fielder could touch it, he wasn't sliding into second with his honed spikes shining in the sun—but he was still the old, the magnificent Georgia Peach.

This is the last chapter of the book, but it cannot

be the last chapter in the story of Tyrus Cobb and baseball.

For wherever baseball is played, minor league or major league, the fans will rise and doff their hats to a new hero, fleet of foot and quick with the bat, but when they come to measure his greatness they will inevitably use as the yardstick the accomplishments of the inimitable Georgia Peach, Tyrus Raymond Cobb. And, it is not likely that this immortal of the diamond will ever be surpassed as an all around player.

LIFETIME RECORD: TYRUS RAYMOND COBB

Born December 18, 1886, Narrows, Banks County, Georgia

Died July 17, 1961, Atlanta, Georgia

Batted left and threw right

YEAR	CLUB	LEAGUE	POS.	GAMES	HR.	RBI.	AVG.
1905	Detroit	American	OF	41	1		.240
1906	"	"	"	97	1		.320
1907	"	"	"	150	5	116	.350
1908	"	"	"	150	4	101	.324
1909	"	"	"	156	9	115	.377
1910	"	"	"	140	8	88	.385
1911	"	"	"	146	8	144	.420
1912	"	"	"	140	7	90	.410
1913	"	"	2-OF	122	4	65	.390
1914	"	"	OF	97	2	57	.368
1915	"	"	"	156	3	95	.370
1916	"	"	"	145	5	67	.371
1917	"	"	"	152	7	108	.383
1918	"	"	1-OF	111	3	64	.382
1919	"	"	OF	124	1	69	.384
1920	"	"	"	112	2	63	.334
1921	"	"	"	128	12	101	.389
1922	"	"	"	137	4	99	.401
1923	"	"	"	145	6	88	.340
1924	"	"	"	155	4	74	.338
1925	"	"	"	121	12	102	.378
1926	"	"	"	79	4	62	.339
1927	Philadelphia	"	"	134	5	93	.357
1928	"	"	"	95	1	40	.323

Major League Totals .... 3033 118 1901 .367

Elected to Hall of Fame, 1936

Index

213

215

POCKET BOOKS

ARCHWAY
PAPERBACKS

Other titles you will enjoy

29553 JACKIE ROBINSON OF THE BROOKLYN DODGERS, by Milton J. Shapiro. Illustrated with photographs. The courageous black man who broke the color line in professional baseball and became one of the all-time greats of the Brooklyn Dodgers. (75¢)

29594 THE JIM THORPE STORY: *America's Greatest Athlete,* by Gene Schoor. Illustrated with photographs. The greatest all-around athlete of this century and his spectacular record in football, baseball, field and track. (75¢)

29331 THE STRANGE INTRUDER, by Arthur Catherall. A reign of terror grips a remote, storm-lashed island when a dangerous invader comes ashore. (60¢)

29332 THE DEVIL AND DANIEL WEBSTER *and Other Stories,* by Stephen Vincent Benét. Illustrated by Harold Denison and Charles Child. Three short stories by the American master of fantasy, folk humor, and irresistible tall tales. (60¢)

(If your bookseller does not have the titles you want, you may order them by sending the retail price, plus 25¢ for postage and handling to: Mail Service Department, POCKET BOOKS, a division of Simon & Schuster, Inc., 1 West 39th Street, New York, N. Y. 10018. Please enclose check or money order—do not send cash.)

29606